Little Music Lessons for Kids

Five Sweet Stories about the Musical Notes, Piano Keyboard, Treble Clef and Musical Staff

Tatiana Bandurina

ISBN-13: 978-1494393700

ISBN-10: 1494393700

CONTENTS

Little Music Lessons for Kids

Lesson 1
A Fascinating Story about the Staff and Treble Clef

Tatiana Bandurina

CONTENTS

This is our home.

And this is my family.

We all love music.

Mother plays the piano.

Dad plays the cello.

Kelly plays the violin.

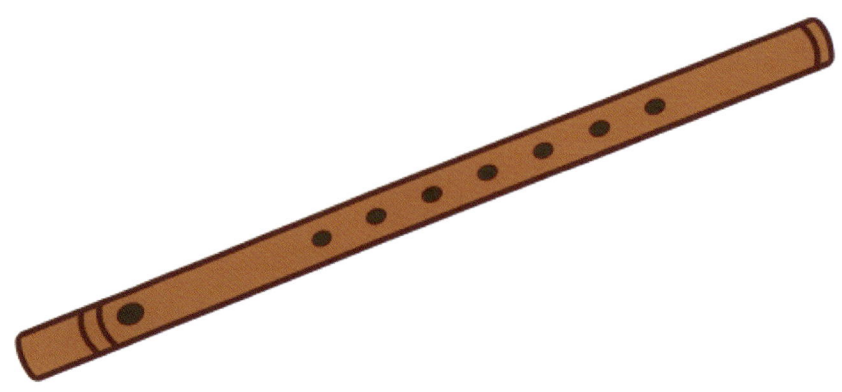

And little Edward plays the flute.

This is me. Everybody calls me a musical puppy, because I know a lot of fascinating stories about music.

I'm very curious. I wonder how adults, looking at a book without pictures, are able to tell stories and fairy-tales? As it turns out, they know all the letters of the alphabet and know how to read!

I'm still small and cannot read. I know only a few letters. But I can count to ten! You know how to count to ten too? Excellent!

In our musical family, there is something new and interesting every day.

And if you know how to count to ten, you ought to know my first story.

Once I learned that music, as well as interesting stories, appears from books.

Stories are written with letters, and music is written with special musical characters called notes.

Musical notes live in a fabulous musical house.

So, once upon a time there was a fabulous house, called the staff. It looks so funny! Look out!

See these lines? Each line is one floor in the musical house.

How many stories do you see? Do the math! Count from the bottom to the top:

One, two, three, four, five! See that? It's easy! One, two, three, four, five!

Hmm ... Wait a minute ... I have seen this somewhere, but where?

I remember! Do you see the hand?

Let's count the fingers on it:

One, two, three, four, five! And now again, count the floors on the staff: One, two, three, four, five!

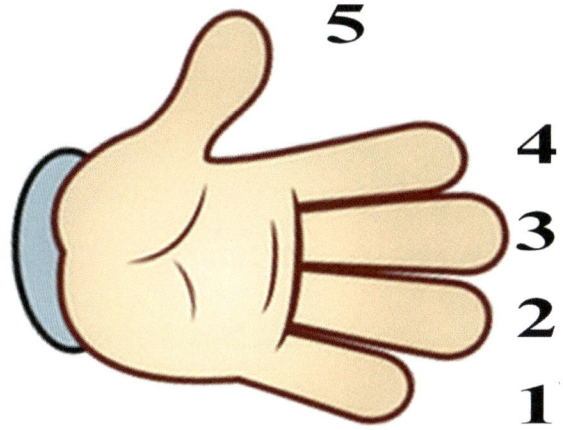

And now again, count the floors on the staff: One, two, three, four, five!

See how they seem to follow the same order?

How many fingers are on your left hand? Do the math! Count form the bottom to the top. One, two, three, four, five. How many fingers are on your right hand?

One, two, three, four, five! Great job!

And now count the floors in the music house again:

One, two, three, four, five!

Excellent!

Now you know that the music house has five floors, and they should be counted from the bottom to the top, like real stories in this house where people live:

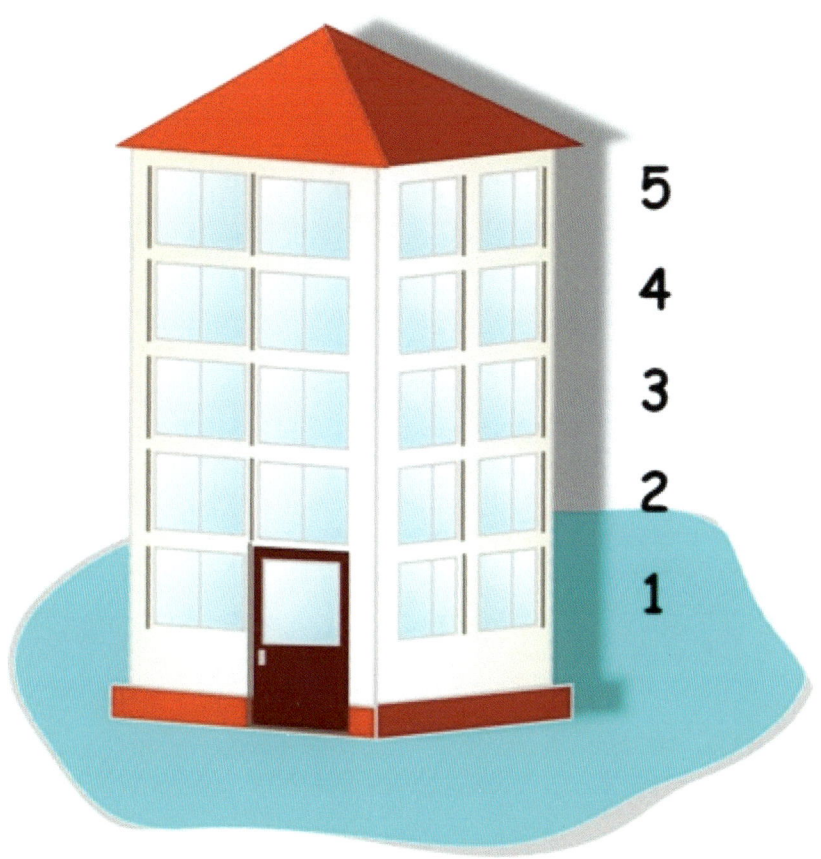

We have a music house — the staff, but where are the people - the musical notes?

Wait a minute! I forgot! To get to the house and see its inhabitants, we need...

Hmm, if the door to the house is closed, we need ... A key! Right!

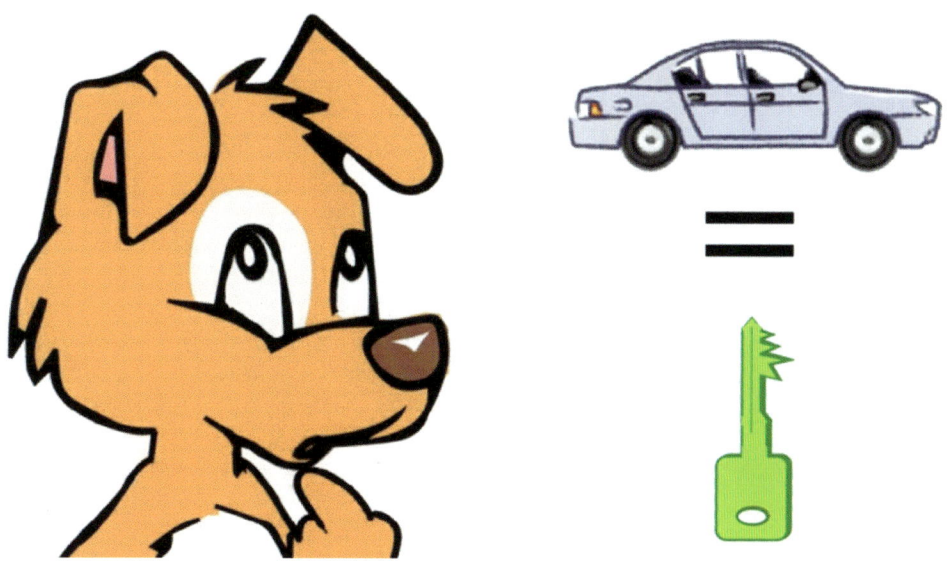

Here's the key to the car…

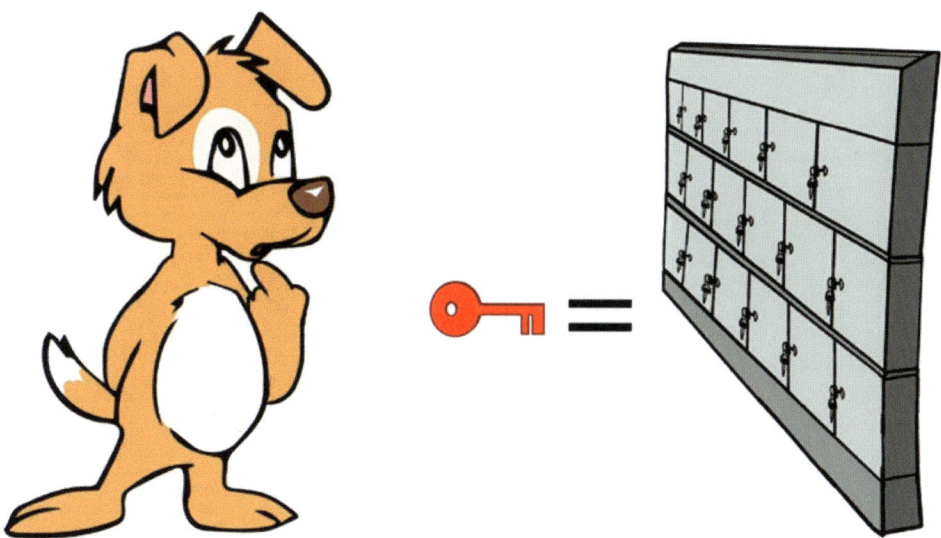

This one is for the mailbox.

This one is for the shed…

This is for something else...

Found it!

Hmm… It does not fit. Strange! This is the key to our house!

I remember! If this is a musical house, we need to have a special musical key. Here it is!

This is called the treble clef or the "G" key!

The treble clef has two tails – a small one and a big one. The small tail clings to one of the lines. What is the story? Which line? Do the math! One... two... The treble clef holds onto the second line!

I'll tell you in confidence who lives on the second line. Note "G" lives on the second line. It looks like an oval. Look again.

Here is the tail of the treble clef. He holds onto the second line, so this clef is called the "G" key.

Now you know what a music house look likes. Its residents are musical notes. I'll remind you that the name of this house is a staff.

Do you remember how many floors there are?

That's right, five!

Now that you know which key opens a music house, or a staff, you know this key is called the Treble Clef or "G" key.

Do you remember why the treble clef is called "G"? Because he holds onto the second line and the note "G" lives on the second line.

Now comes the fun part.

You are already a big boy or girl and know how to tell great stories. Tell the story about the musical house (staff), first to mom, then to dad, then to your favorite toys.

If you have brothers, sisters, or grandparents, be sure to tell this story to them too. And tell them that you will learn how to read music very soon! I will teach you! It's easy!

Next time, I will tell you a story about a boastful snail and a brave fire poker, and teach you to write the treble clef. It is so funny!

See you in the next story!

HOMEWORK FOR PARENTS

Dear parents, please read this book first from the beginning to the end before you show it to your child.

Read it? Excellent!

Now you have a choice of how to use this lesson:

1 Just read the book to the child and show him the pictures.

2 Encourage the child to move while telling the story.

It's very easy to do. Tell your child the story of the musical house and the treble clef using any puppet toy you have at home.

If I had to choose, I would have taken advantage of option number 2. Why?

The secret of this lesson is that when you make the child an active participant in learning, you will automatically initiate one of the "tools" of raising children - imitation. The greater effect on children is not what you say, but what you really show them.

Recommendations

Become a kid! Change your voice - your puppets should not speak in mother's voice. Each should have its own "special" voice.

Once the child sees how you can play with the puppet, which can be a "teacher," he will want to do the same thing that you do in class. If the desire to imitate occurred after the first lesson, it means that you did everything correctly and the child was interested.

The child will always play by imitating you! The child's desire to play with a puppet toy (like you) and repeat the same story in front of the dolls, brother / sister, father, or grandmother will encourage him to practice. This happens quite unbeknownst to him. Encourage him to action!

Frequent repetition will bring the child strong knowledge. The practice will give him great pleasure in what he does.

Even if you do not understand anything about reading and writing of music, you can use this book to teach your child.

First, use this book to introduce your child to a musical family. To expand his horizons, show your child pictures of the musical instruments that which mother, father, daughter and son play.

When I talk about the main narrator (the musical puppy), place the book next to you and use the appropriate puppet toy that is in your home.

Read the book, moving the puppet toy in front of the child. You will find that he will look at just the toy.

Before the lesson, prepare a set of keys, a plain sheet of paper, a ruler and a pencil (or pen or marker). Let your "teacher" draw the staff with a ruler and a pencil. It would be much better if you involve your child and give him the opportunity to draw one or all five straight lines. This is a great opportunity to teach the child to use a ruler and a pencil!

If the child is small (3 or 4 years), you should cherish his ability to concentrate for a short time. That is why you need to have two sheets of paper with drawings:

1 – Your picture of the staff (5 parallel lines)

2 – Your picture with a staff, treble clef and the "G" note.

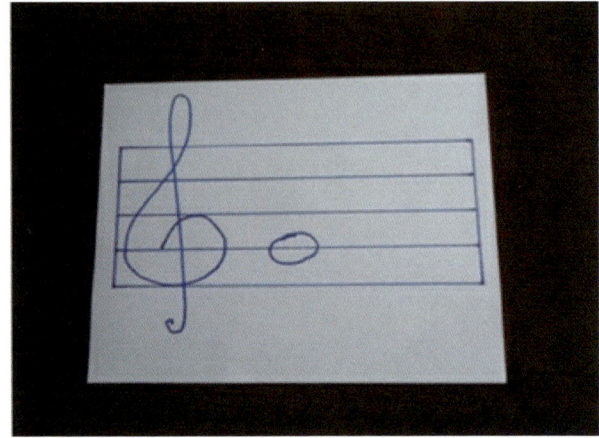

Do not worry if your treble clef does not look very nice. I promise that after the next lesson you will become a master of musical calligraphy!

Keep track of the lesson's time. Your lesson should take no longer than 15 minutes. For this purpose, you can break it into two parts: the first part of the lesson to talk about a staff, and the second part of the lesson to continue the story and talk about the treble clef.

Repetition - the mother of learning. That's why I repeat these names several times in the story: music staff, treble clef or "G" key. Several times I ask the child to count "floors" in the music house to the fingers on the hand. This comparison of the number of lines on the staff and the number of fingers on the child's hand can help kids quickly memorize the learning material. It will help even more if you count your fingers too because that adds to his desire to imitate what you do.

Important!

It is important that the child has learned to tell this story to other members of your family or his toys. Let your kid (just like you) put a puppet toy on his hand and repeat the story that he heard from you.

If a child has a small vocabulary, and he still cannot tell the story in the way it is written in the book, do not worry. The main thing is that during the story the child:

- has learned the exact number of lines on the staff and correctly counted them (bottom to top).

- remember the names of the treble clef and where the "G" note is written.

For his stories, give him your two images, help your child to use them, and the first time you help, recall the words: a staff, treble clef, the "G" note.

After this lesson, continue to motivate the child to practice and help him retain his new knowledge. How? Very simple! Here's what you need to do after the first lesson:

Walking with a child? Ask him to count the floors in this house, and in that, and yet in those… Ask how many floors there are in the music house. What's it name?

Have you found houses in a children's picture book? Let the child count the floors. Getting out a clean spoon from the closet? Set aside five of them. Arrange all five spoons in parallel lines, just like the lines on the staff. Ask your child to count them. Make sure he counted them from the bottom up. Immediately ask how many floors there are in the music house. What's it called?

Come to the door of your house with a child and you want to open it with the key? Ask him what the name of the musical key is that opens a staff.

Thus, you have an opportunity as often as possible to focus the child's attention on new words.

To help the child remember the name of the staff, use it often in your questions. For example: Don't ask, "How many lines in a musical home?" Instead ask, "How many lines in a staff?"

To help the child remember the name of the treble clef or "G" key, also use them in questions. Why is the musical key called "G" key? On what line is "G" written?

The more often the child repeats what he saw and heard, the stronger his memory and knowledge. The stronger his knowledge, the higher his interest in music lessons. Interest - that is what lies at the heart of all learning.

If you use the natural environment for the repetition of what I mentioned above, you'll feel completely calm and the talent of your child will grow before your eyes!

Good luck and see you in the second lesson!

ISBN-13: 978-1494393700

ISBN-10: 1494393700

Little Music Lessons for Kids

Lesson 2
Learning How to Write a Treble Clef - A Funny Story about the Boastful Snail and Brave Fire Poker

Tatiana Bandurina

CONTENTS

Hi! I am a musical puppy. I know a lot of interesting musical stories.

Last time I showed you the house where music lives. Its name is the staff.

The staff opens with a special key, called a treble clef or "G" key.

I already know how to write a treble clef, and today I'll teach you how to do it. But first, listen to my new musical history. It happened in our living room. There is a large fireplace and an aquarium there.

Once, on an early winter morning, I overheard a conversation between a snail and a fire poker.

The snail is a very hard worker. It lives in our aquarium with fish and cleans its glass walls, so we can see the fish well, and the fish can see us too.

The fire poker lives near a fireplace. It is also a hard worker, and it is very brave.

The fire poker has a very dangerous job. It often has to go into the fire to move the wood in the fireplace.

So, I heard the snail and the fire poker arguing with each other. They tried to find out which of them is more beautiful.

The dispute began with the snail.

"I'm so cute! Look! I have a beautiful house! It has many flourishes!"

And the snail turned so that everybody could see her beautiful house.

"I am long and slender. I do not need your curls!" said the poker proudly, and straightened more.

But the snail did not bother, and, looking slowly at the fire poker from bottom to top, said:

"You're too long and too smooth! With such growth, it is simply impossible to hide in a house like mine! Oh yes, I forgot that you do not have a house!"

And the snail laughed aloud:

"Ha-ha-ha! You are homeless! And I have a house! Look out!" And the snail immediately hid in its house.

I liked the snail house so much I wanted to draw its portrait. I took a piece of paper and a pencil. Then I put the pencil in the middle of a paper and began to draw a curl without lifting the pencil from the paper.

Look, I got a snails' house!

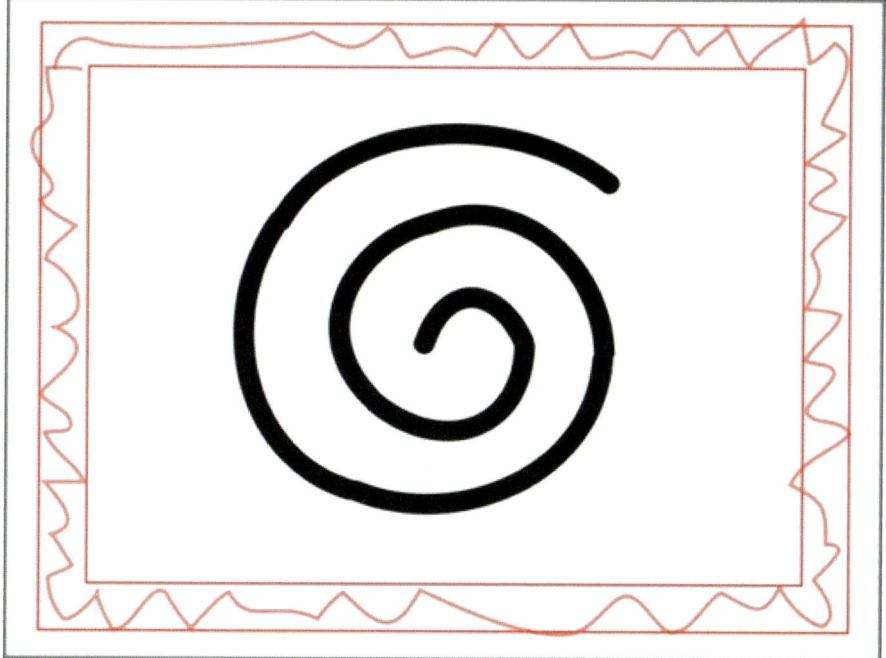

I was so engrossed in drawing the house that I did more portraits of it. On those portraits, the snail house was big and small.

But the story about the snail and fire poker is not over yet. Hear more ...

All day the fire poker sadly sighed and pondered the words of the snail.

The snail was right: the fire poker didn't have a house. It has worked in the fireplace, but could not live there because it was very hot.

The fire poker was very frustrated that everybody could call it "homeless." All its thoughts were focused on where to find its own house. And suddenly, the fire poker got a great idea:

"If I cannot find a house," it said, "I can make the same whorl, which a snail has!"

At this time, Daddy went to the fireplace. He put the fire poker in the fireplace and moved the fire wood for a very long time. Staying in the fire, the lower part of the fire poker heated and become soft.

When Daddy put the fire poker in its regular place, its long leg bent at the bottom.

I liked the fire poker's new look so I drew its portrait. First I drew a long straight line like this:

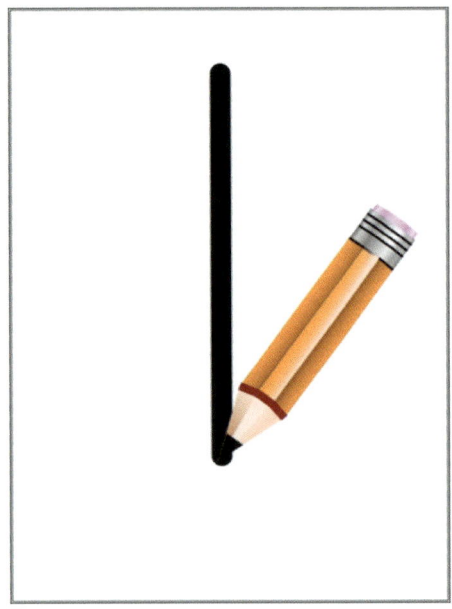

And then I turned it slightly to the left like this:

The fire poker, seeing its new leg with a curl, was very happy.

Success greatly inspired the fire poker, and the next time Daddy went to the fireplace, the fire poker stuck its head in the fire and held it there as long as it could.

After returning from the fire, and becoming soft again, the fire poker made an even greater effort and bent its head like this:

The snail was very scared.

I was surprised by the courage of the fire poker.

Even the greatest desire could not make me stick a paw in the fire! I drew a new portrait of fire poker.

Let's see how I did it: that's his bent head:

It is a straight body:

And this is a bent leg.

These days the snail has stopped bragging and the fire poker is no longer working in the fireplace.

Of course, a bent fire poker is not much use in the fireplace, but perhaps it is useful somewhere else?

I decided to connect the two portraits: the snail's house and the new fire poker.

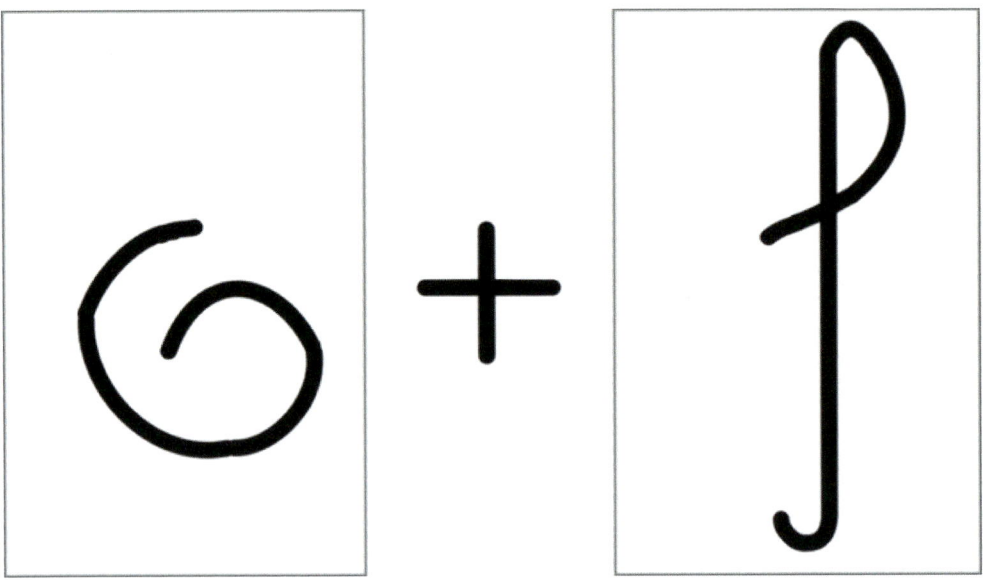

Here's a snail's house.

And this is the head of a bold poker.

Here is the leg.

And we've got a ...

Treble clef or "G" key!

Now I'll try to do the same on the staff.

I put the pencil on the second line and start drawing snail's house.

Then I gently touch the third line.

Now I gently touch a first line and continue to draw a snail's house and stop on the fourth line.

At this point I begin to draw a portrait of the fire poker. Here is its bent head.

Here is his straight body.

And here is his leg with a curl.

See how it is nice and simple?

I hope you liked my story about a brave fire poker and the boastful snail! What about the portraits I have drawn?

Tell this story to Mommy, Dad, your brother or sister, or even your grandparents, if you have them. Draw the snails' house, and two portraits of the new fire poker. Then draw a treble clef, and put this drawing on the wall in your room.

Next time, I'll introduce you to notes. In that story, you'll learn how they chose their "music apartment." I'll teach you to be friends with them.

Meet you in the next story!

HOMEWORK FOR PARENTS

I hope that you, dear parents, liked my story about a snail and a fire poker too. Now is the time to work a bit.

One of the first difficulties in the classroom is to read and write music – to get writing skills and learn how to write a treble clef. Children do manage this task with great difficulty.

I think that parents who never studied music and who purchased Lesson Number 1 of the series Little Music Lessons for Kids already know about that. In that one, you had to draw a treble clef without any hints!

Now, let's get together to help your child get the skill of writing a treble clef and increase the interest of your son or daughter in reading and writing musical notations.

Lesson Two has a lot of work that requires personal involvement of the child. Therefore, we'll split this lesson into parts.

So, first read the story to a child from beginning to the end, carefully considering each picture with him. You may have read this story several times before a child picks up a pencil. The younger he is, the longer he will need with the story and the pictures.

Now firmly remember:

The writing part of the lesson should last no more than 10-15 minutes! As I said above, break the tasks into parts - two, three, or even more. For example:

1 - The child learns to write the 1st part of the treble clef, drawing the snail's house on a white sheet of paper.

2 - The child learns to write part of the treble clef, a straight line with the curl at the bottom.

3 – The child learns to write the "head" of the treble clef.

4 - The child learns to write part of the treble clef (the snail's house) on the staff.

5 - The child learns to write the second part of the treble clef, as shown in the picture.

6 - The child learns to write a whole treble clef, without lifting the pencil from the paper.

How many parts should you split the lesson into? Should you split it at all?

It depends on the following factors: the age of your child, his attention span, his ability to concentrate and other existing skills of your child.

What if all the tasks are very easy for the child? That is great! It indicates high intelligence and good coordination between the eye and the hand. Keep tracking the success of your child and praise him for his hard work.

Let him learn to write beautifully, accurately and ... quickly. For this purpose, you need *Blank Music Paper for Kids*.

You can buy colored printed *Blank Music Paper for Kids* that are ready to use here: http://www.amazon.com/dp/1483946703

After purchasing this, you'll get 27 blank music papers. The first eight of them are for little kids and for those who are just starting to practice musical notation. On those pages, you'll find three staffs. The width between the lines of the staffs should be comfortable for beginners.

The other manuscripts, respectively, have narrower line spacing staves. They are for increasing the skills in musical calligraphy.

Recommendations

Divide the practical part of the lesson into parts and teach it over several days. Do not force a child to do the job in one day! (Unless he is a child prodigy)! Remember that a child should PLAY AND LEARN.

When you give the task to the child, instead of saying, "Write that part of the treble clef," it is better to lean on the content of the story and ask him to draw:

The house of a snail, the new leg of the fire poker with swirls, a new head of the fire poker, and the fire poker with new curls.

Necessary!

Give the child a chance to show his drawings to his Daddy (mother, grandmother, grandfather). I assure you, learning how to write a treble clef is a very difficult job for a little child, so you and all the other family members should encourage his hard work.

You should remind your child to tell this story to your relatives. Ask him to paint portraits of the snail's house and the fire poker during the story. Do not judge his work. If the first pictures are not perfect; it is better encourage the child to tell the story several times.

If you do not have many people who want to listen to your child, let the child tell the story to you a few times. Make it easy. Here are the options for motivation:

- Sorry, honey, I forgot why snail praised its house? What was beautiful in it? Can you draw it for me?

- Remind me, please, what's wrong with the fire poker, after she had been in the fire? Can you draw it for me?

- I loved the story about the snail and the fire poker! Tell it to me one more time, please!

- You tell the story so well! Tell me one more time!

- Your portraits of the snail and fire poker are so beautiful! Draw them for me again!

Remember this: Repetition is the mother of learning.

Instead of boring practice, make the child a major participant in a fascinating story. If you continue the tradition that began in the first lesson and decide to lead the second lesson with a puppet toy (we talked about it in the previous lesson), let the puppet draw the pictures of the musical puppy using a pencil or marker. Believe that all your hard work will be rewarded.

Here are some examples:

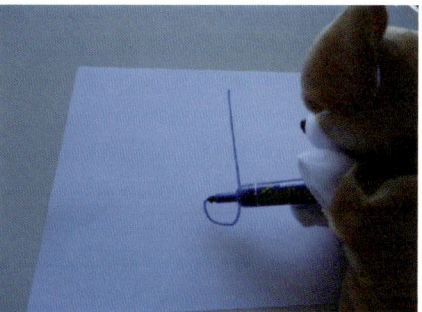

The child will want to write the treble clef like a musical puppy did it in the story!

Overcome Additional Challenges

Often, young children have not yet developed enough eye-hand coordination to repeat even the simplest pattern. Do not be upset. To help a child with such problems, first draw one part of a treble clef with dashed lines (prepare several variants, so he can practice). Let him try to write a treble clef by tracing and connecting the dashes. (That is, with a "hint.")

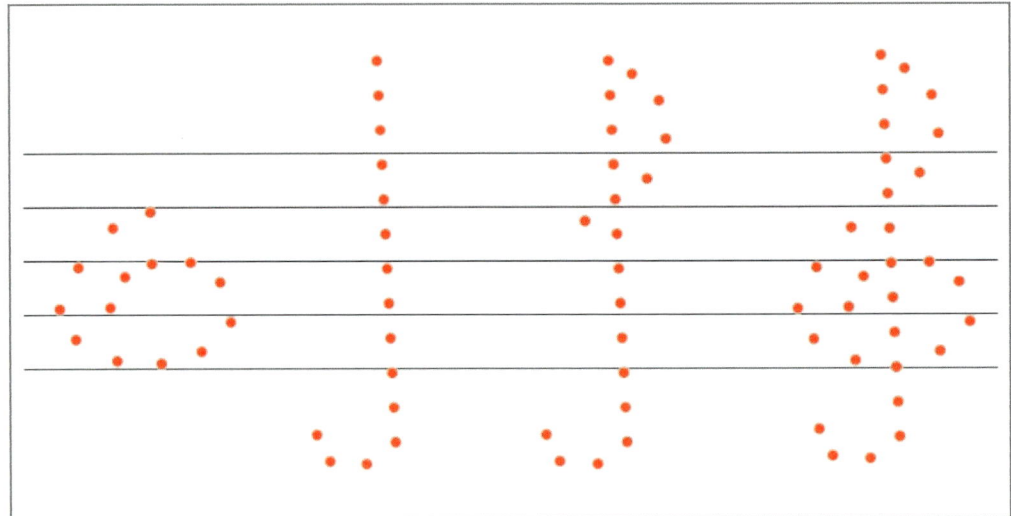

When the child gets some experience doing it that way, let him try to draw this part of the treble clef without hinting; that is, without the dotted lines. When he has mastered that, move on to the next part of the treble clef.

In Lesson 3, your child will learn about the names of musical notes and where the notes are written on the staff. He will also improve his musical skills of calligraphy and his eye-hand coordination.

See you in the next lesson!

ISBN-13: 978-1494393700

ISBN-10: 1494393700

Little Music Lessons for Kids

Lesson 3
Learning the Line Notes
A Story about How Musical Notes Got their Apartments

Tatiana Bandurina

CONTENTS

Hi! I am a musical puppy.

You probably already know my story about a music house - a staff. Do you remember how the boastful snail and brave fire poker taught you to write a treble clef? Great!

Today, I'll introduce you to people staff – musical notes.

To get acquainted with musical notes, we need the first seven letters of the alphabet, which I heard in the ABC song:
A, b, c, d, e, f, g

These are the names of the notes!

All you need to do - is to repeat the first line of a song and you will learn their names very quickly.

Now I will tell you a new story ...

When the music staff (Music House) was built, only one note lived there. It was the note "G".

She was very sad and boring living without friends and neighbors, so she wrote the ad:

"Musical Apartments for Sale. Refer to the note "G" at music staff."

After 30 seconds thinking, the note "G" wrote another ad:

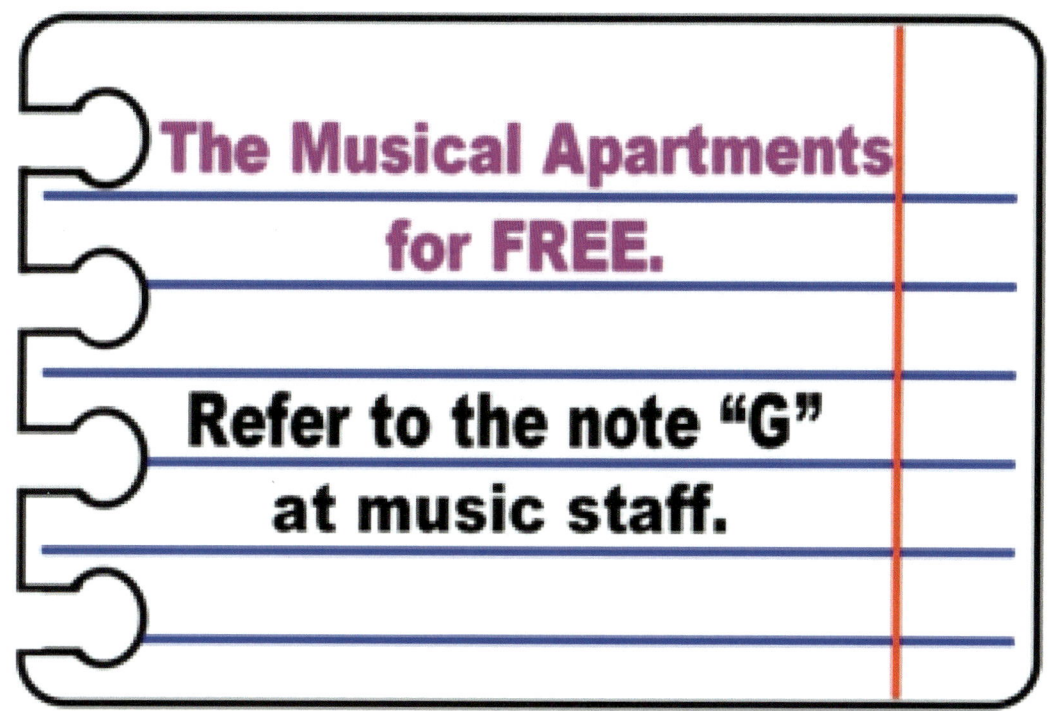

Carefully, she read the ad several times and, making sure that there were no errors, the note "G" hung it wherever she could: on the trees, cars, houses - and even the flowers.

Other homeless notes, reading the ad, immediately rushed to take seats on the staff and, in a few minutes, all five floors were occupied.

Here's how it happened:

Note "**E**" was very **E**ager. Seeing that the second line was busy (after all, note "**G**" lived there!), she was afraid that she might be left without a music apartment and quickly took the first floor - the first line.

The note **"B"** loved to be the center of attention, so she sat down on the third line.

Here is the resident of the fourth line - this is the note "**D**", she loves **D**ancing.

And, finally seeing number five on the fifth line, the note "**F**" screamed: "Number **F**ive! This is my **F**avorite number! ".

She immediately took her musical apartment.

Time passed and one day the note **"B"**, who lived on the third line, started thinking:

"I was very lucky that I took the center of the staff. It happened because I am the most intelligent. My name is **"B"**. **"B"** is the first letter in the word

Big

It means I should be bigger than other notes. I must be the biggest and, if I'm the biggest, it means that I'm the most important here!"

Imaging that all the other notes will respect her, the note **"B"** swelled like a balloon and took place from the second to the fourth line, like this:

Do you know what the other notes did when they saw the note **"B"**? Right! They did not become friends with her because she took up so much space on the staff!

Note **"B"** was very upset that her plan failed.

She was most upset that the other notes have turned away from her and did not talk to her.

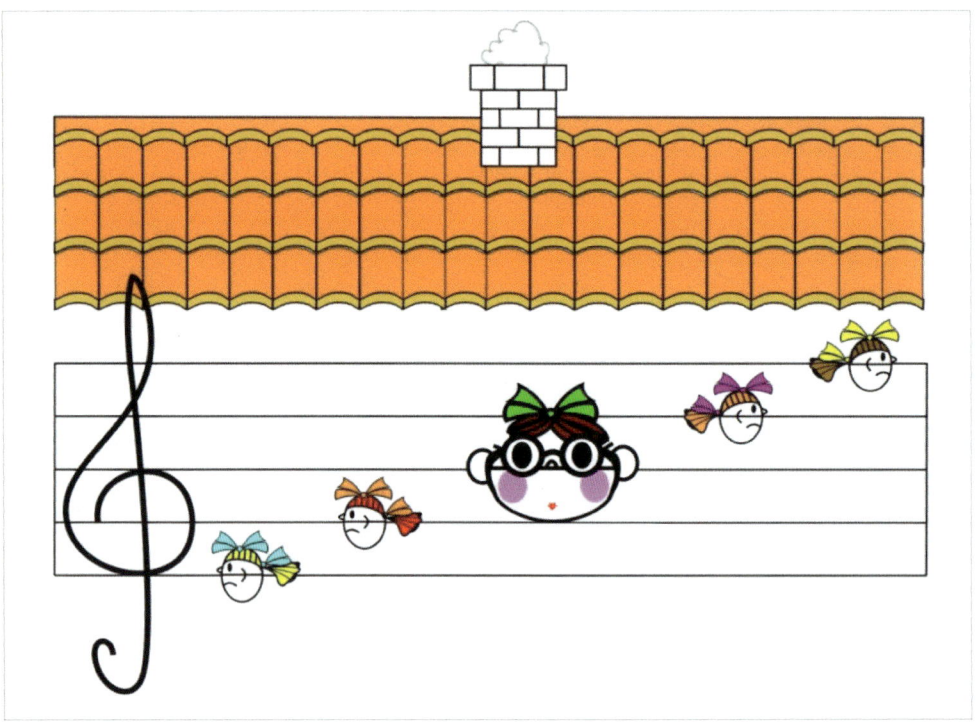

Note **"B"** had to release excess air to be blown away and become the same size as the other notes.

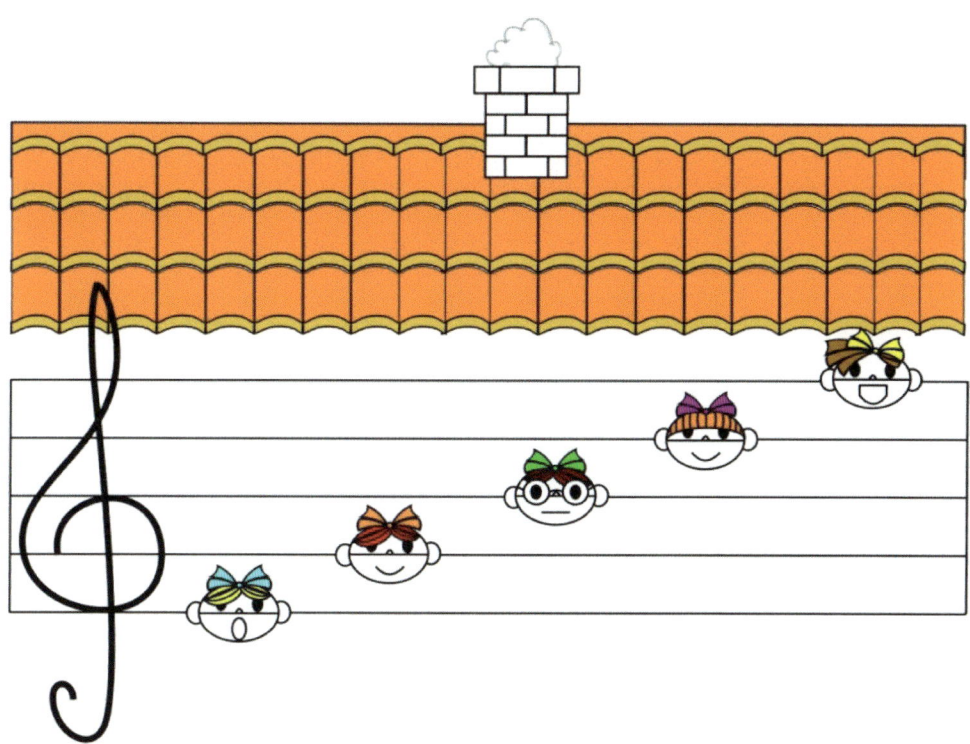

From that day, peace and order reigned on the staff.

Pay attention to the fact that all of the notes that live in this house are very neat, and most importantly - honest. They do not take other neighbor's storeys and each of them lives only on their line.

Of course, everyone wants to be friends with them, right?

A STAFF

Now I will show you how you can play with the notes that you already know.

For this game, we need a ring.

Imagine that this is a staff and a ring is a "note."

Put your "note" on the second finger from the bottom.

And we get ... Note "**G**"! Say "**G**"!

Do you remember the most eager musical note? On which finger should we put the ring?

Right! The first! Note **"E"** lives on the first line.

Here are the notes that live on the ground and second floor:

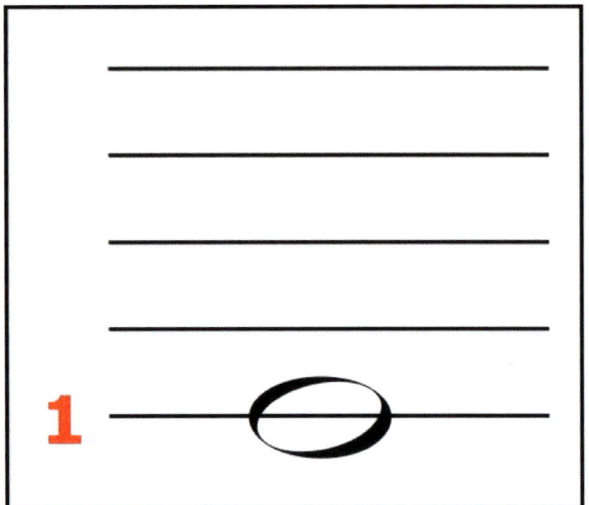
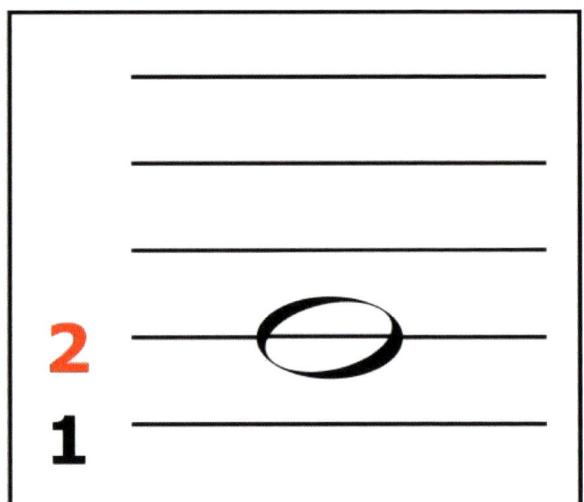

Here are the notes that live on the third and fourth floor:

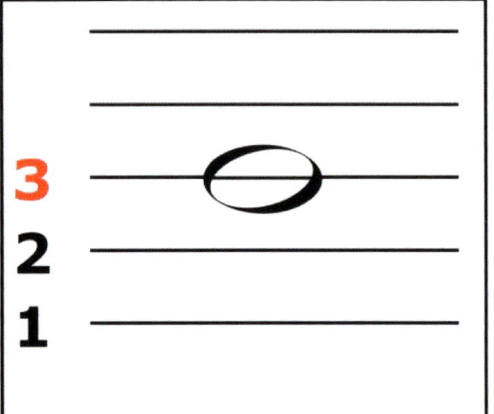
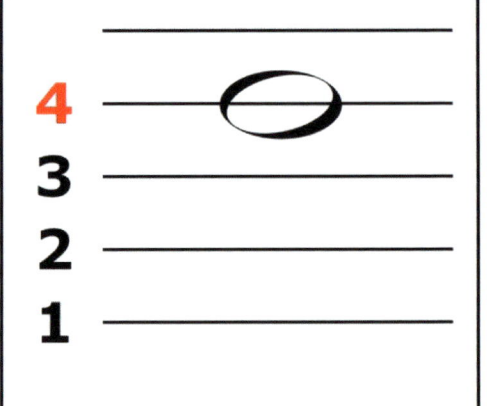

And here is the note that lives on the fifth floor:

Now take another look at the staff and the music notes that are living on the lines: on the first, on the second, the third, the fourth and on the fifth.

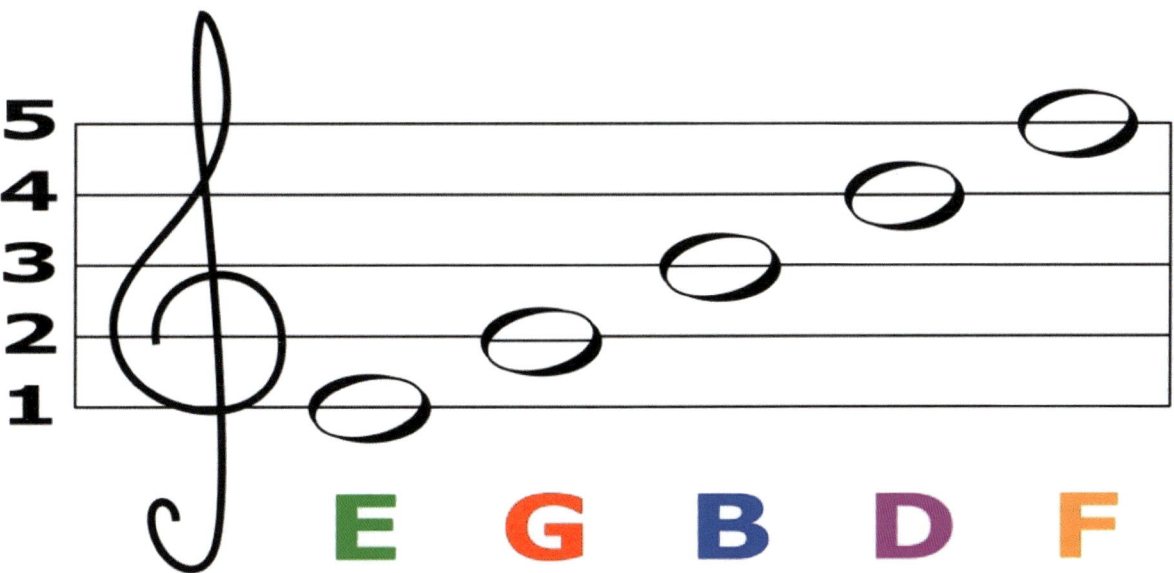

See that? Each of these musical notes lives on its line and does not stick to the adjacent note.

After listening to this story, ask your mom for a special piece of paper on which there is a staff, or several staffs and a marker or pencil.

Draw your music house residents who live on each floor, but do not forget to write at the beginning of the staff the "**G**" key.

This should be done every time you are going to write notes on the staff.

When you write all the notes on the lines, teach to do it everyone you know - a brother, sister, father, grandmother, grandfather or friend.

Be an attentive teacher and see that your students write notes on the rulers as carefully as you do. If they draw an "inflated" note, tell them that no one will be friends with it, because it takes up too much space.

Next time I will tell you my new story about what other musical notes did when they read the announcement, came, and saw that all the music apartments were occupied.

Meet you in the next story!

HOMEWORK FOR PARENTS

Dear Parents, you need to know a simple rule: all musical notes, regardless of musical keys are line or space notes.

Depending on the age of the child and his or her abilities, this topic can be explained entirely, and can be divided into two parts, which I did in this (third) and will continue in the next (fourth) lesson.

Children - and even adults - learn faster when they have practical exercises. Therefore, after theoretical familiarity with reading notes on the lines (the story of how musical notes occupied apartments), I suggest your child take active steps, during which he can apply the theoretical knowledge in practice.

I recommend your son or daughter play the game of putting musical notes (ring) on the staff (the fingers of the hand).

The palm of the child best demonstrates the staff, and a wedding (or any other) ring is a perfect example of the musical notes.

Sometimes, children (especially young children) cannot understand the meaning of a note on the line. By placing a ring onto their fingers, one by one, they easily learn the concept of "on the line".

If your child is familiar with the musical stories from the first two lessons, it is good to know that the line stave is considered only from the bottom up, and that the note "G" is written on the second line.

Before you go for practical training (playing with the ring), read the story to your child at least two times.

Playing the game with a ring and recalling the content of today's stories, will quickly and easily help your child to remember where the written notes E, G, B, D and F sit on the stave. For example, ask him to show where the note "F" lives.

If you see that a child is having difficulty answering, instead of calling the fifth line (or touching his thumb), it is better to remind him that the note "F", seeing his line, shouted: "My favorite number!". Ask your child: What is the favorite number of the note "F"? That's right, five! Where should you put on the "note"? That's right, the uppermost finger!

Please ensure that your child is always holding his palm to his face! Here's another example:

Ask your child:

"Do you remember the note, who decided that she was the main note on the staff? What's her name? Show me the line on which she lives! Put this "note" on the correct "line".

Make sure that the child is wearing the ring on the right (middle) finger.

Children often write notes on the lines in different sizes during early lessons. It happens because they are not able to focus on the staff. The story about the "inflated note B," which I thought up, helps your child to focus on making the notes the same size.

Recommendations

To get a good result, it is sufficient to play this game with your child at least once a day for 3-5 minutes. Allow your child to wear a "notes" ring, or place it on your fingers or those of other people your child knows.

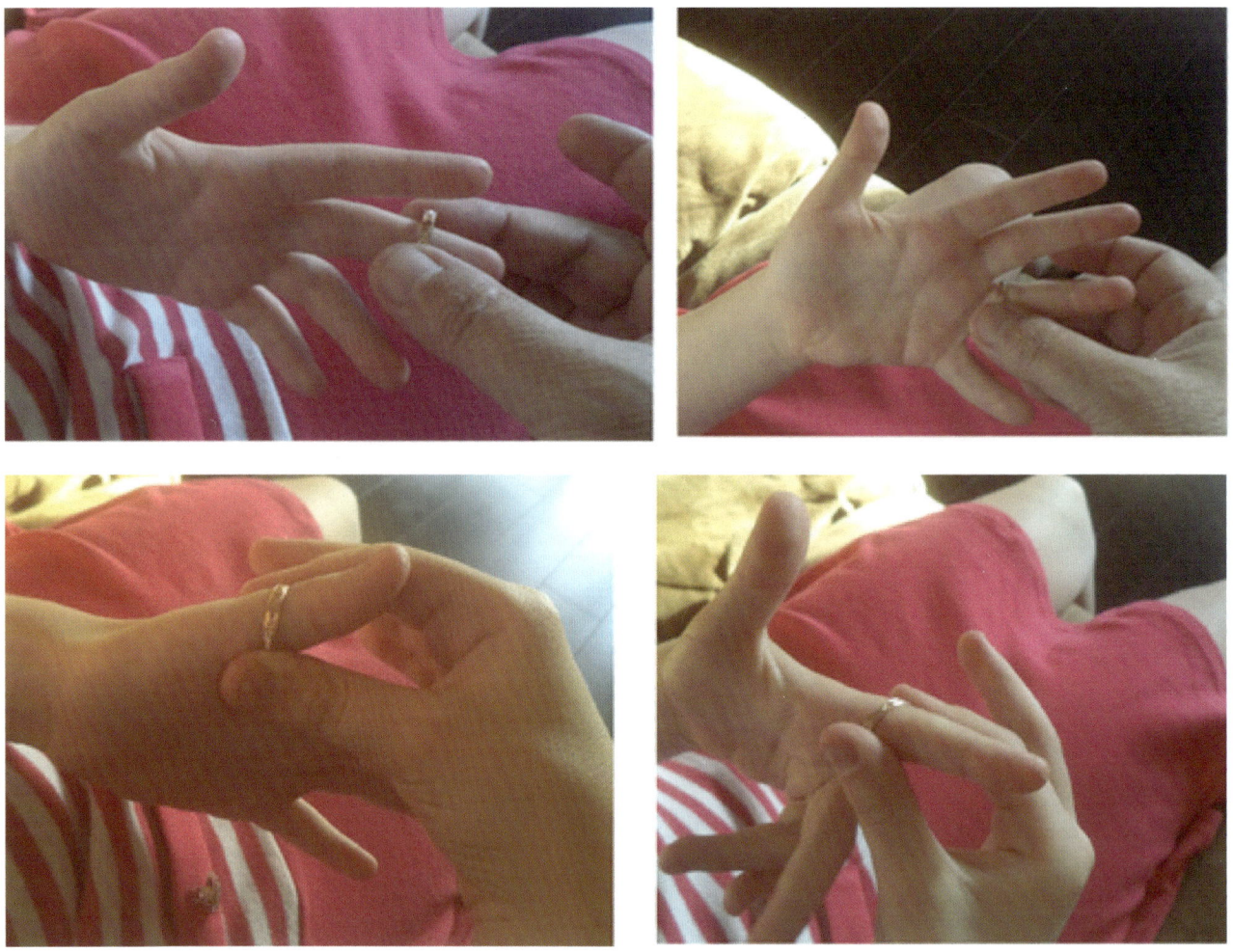

When the little one remembers the location of the musical notes well, he can practice writing them on the staff. Ask him to do it, calling out the notes in different sequences.

For this practical exercise, you can buy colored printed *Blank Music Paper for Kids* that are **ready to use** here: http://www.amazon.com/dp/1483946703

Important!

There is another simple, but strict, rule. The "G" key "opens" **each** musical line. Only after that can you, or your child, write notes on this staff! Make sure that your little one always carries out this important rule.

If your child is unable to write the "G' key, just read him the story about boastful snail and brave fire poker from **Lesson No 2** in the series *Little Music Lessons for Kids*. This funny story will teach your son, or daughter, to write the "G" key very easily.

It is also very useful if a child learns a song about the alphabet which has the names of all seven musical notes (even if he will learn only the first line of the song: A, B, C, D, E, F, G).

In the next lesson, your child will learn about the notes that are written between the lines (space notes), as well as those that are written above and below the lines, to get acquainted with the notes on an extra line.

Further memorable stories and practical exercises are waiting for your child. They will help him learn to easily read and write music!

Little Music Lessons for Kids

Lesson 4

Learning the Space Musical Notes:
The Story of Musical Notes from the Beauty Salon

By Tatiana Bandurina

Little Music Lessons for Kids

Lesson 4
Learning the Space Musical Notes
The Story of Musical Notes from the Beauty Salon

TATIANA BANDURINA

CONTENTS

Hi! It's me again, your little friend—the musical puppy.

Last time, I told you the story about how music notes occupied floors in a musical house (the lines on the staff), remember? Today, I'll tell you the continuation of this amazing story.

So, the first five notes saw note G's advertisement and read it. They took their musical apartments very quickly. Within a short time, all the lines on the staff were full. But other musical notes didn't know about the ad. They stayed in the city as well and also wanted to have their own house because they had nowhere to live.

The day after the ad appeared in the streets of the city, I saw four musical notes in the beauty salon. They were very busy.

These musical notes wanted to make their faces the most beautiful in the city. To do this, they painted on eyelashes, lips, cheeks, eyebrows and even put on face powder. When they finished their make-up, the musical notes started to show off in front of each other and praise each other:

- "Oh, honey, you have the most beautiful, long, black eyelashes!"

- "And you, my dear, have very red lips!"

- "No one is able to trace beautiful eyebrows like you. They are so pretty!"

And so on...

From morning till night, these four musical notes spent their time at the beauty salon, unaware of what was happening outside the window.

Suddenly, one of the musical notes—the one who had the most beautiful eyes—saw a car outside. This car had an ad already familiar to you. After reading the ad, the note shouted:

- "Oh! I also want to have my own apartment! Perhaps there are lot of tenants in this musical house! I can show my beautiful eyes to all the neighbors and they can appreciate them!

The musical note immediately jumped out of the beauty salon and raced to occupy the apartment. The remaining three notes hurried after her.

Upon arrival, our beauty notes sadly noticed that all of the floors in the house were occupied by the other musical notes. But they also wanted to live on the staff very much!

Finally, the first musical note, who had the most beautiful eyes, noticed a window between the first and second floors. She made her way back and opened the window. Then she stuck her handsome face under the gentle rays of the sun. The musical note said, smiling happily:

- "Oh, how nice!"

Seeing the beautiful face of a friend sticking out of the window, the other three beauties found three more windows between the floors of musical house and also poked their faces out, showing them to the sun (and to the neighbors, too!).

The second note moved between the second and third floors.

The third one occupied the place between the third and fourth floors,

and the fourth one took up position between the fourth and fifth levels.

The new inhabitants figured out that they could live between the lines. They also loved to show off their beautiful faces, so they called their friendship union a FACE. They did not have names and each of them decided to take one letter from the word FACE. Now we can read their names:

Here's musical note F,

this one is A,

A

this is C,

C

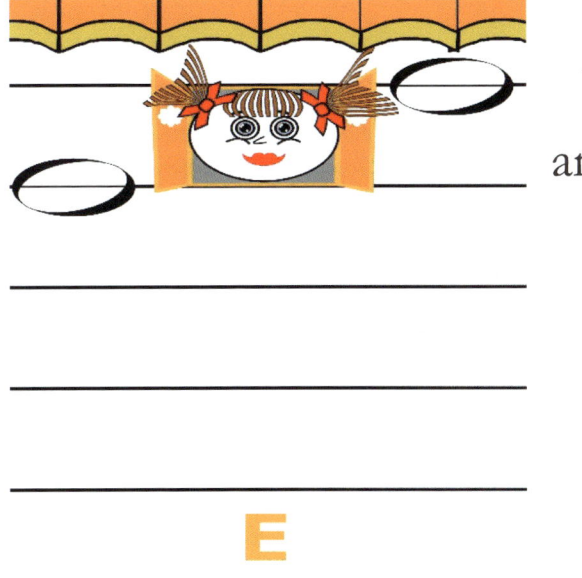

and this one E.

Have you ever seen people living in homes between floors? Ha - ha - ha! Of course not; but this is a magic house and, therefore, there can be all sorts of miracles.

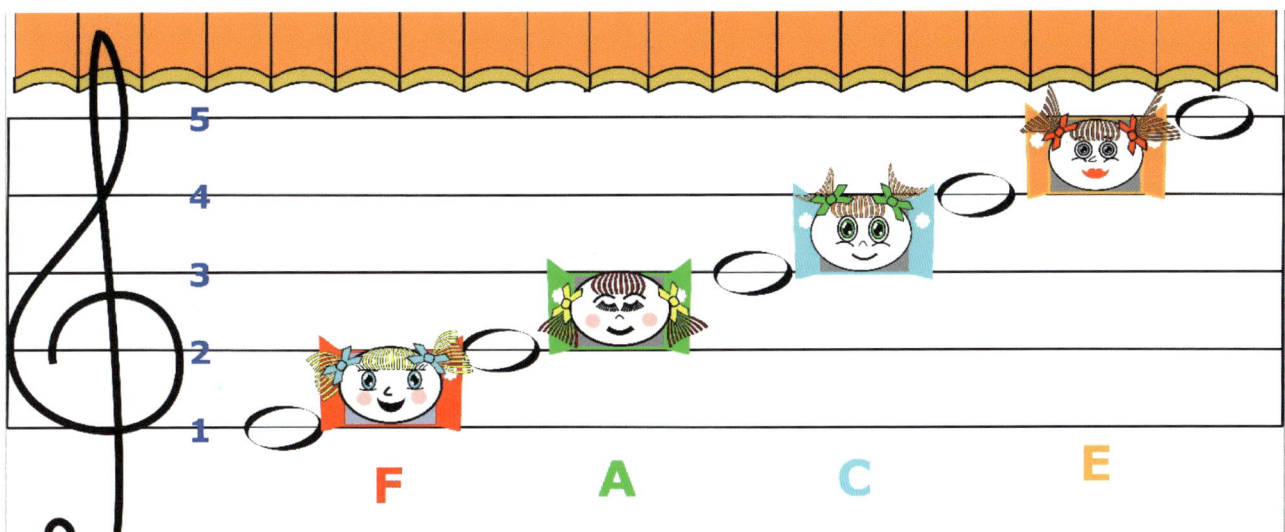

And now we write all the musical notes in the order in which they are located on the staff.

Let's start with the musical notes that first settled on the staff and have taken all the lines. I will write them far away from each other, and leave space for the notes which live between the floors. To make notes clearly visible on the lines, I will write them in black. Here you are.

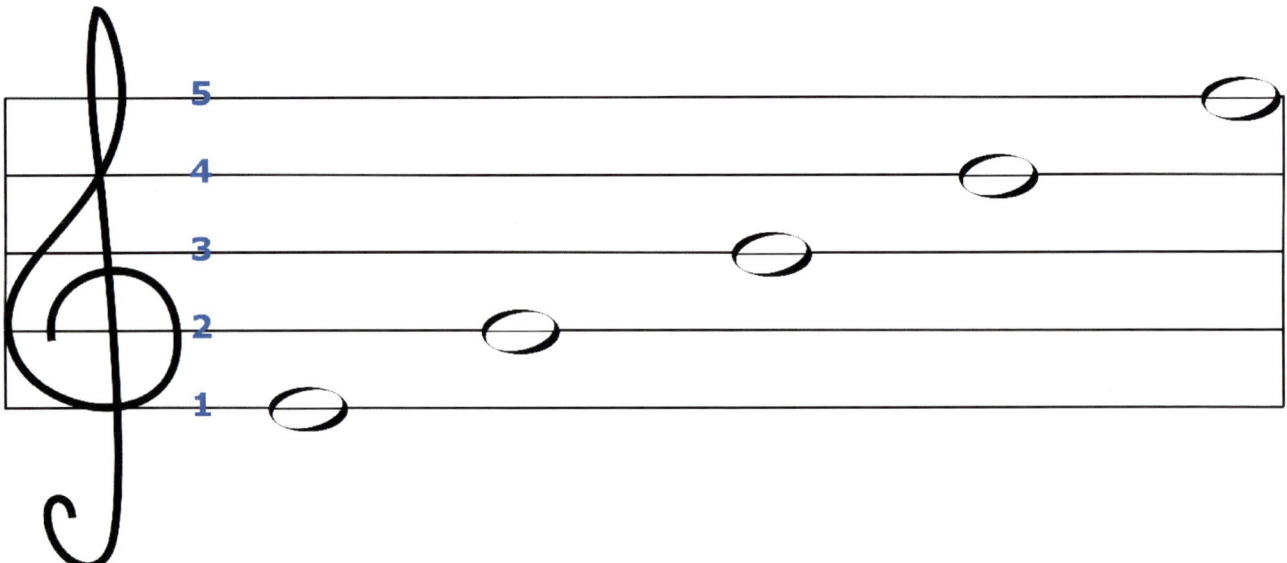

And now I'll write down the notes that live between the floors. They are written between lines. Look:

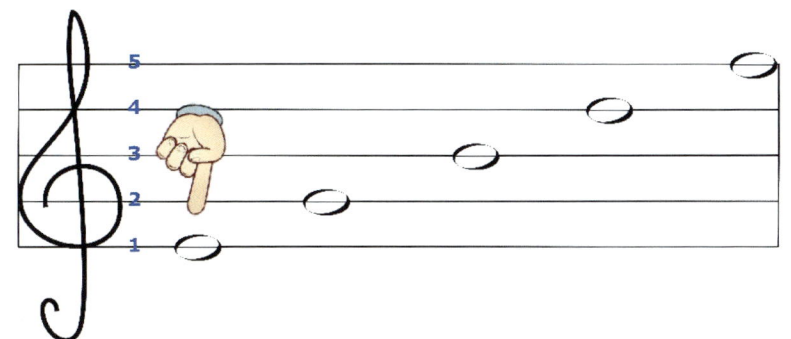

Here's the note "E." She lives on the first line,

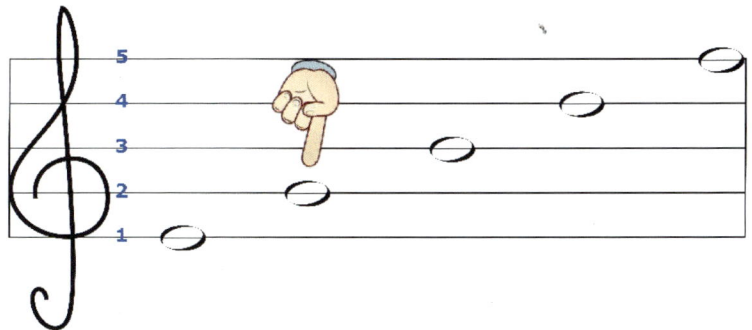

and this is "G." Her apartment is on the second line,

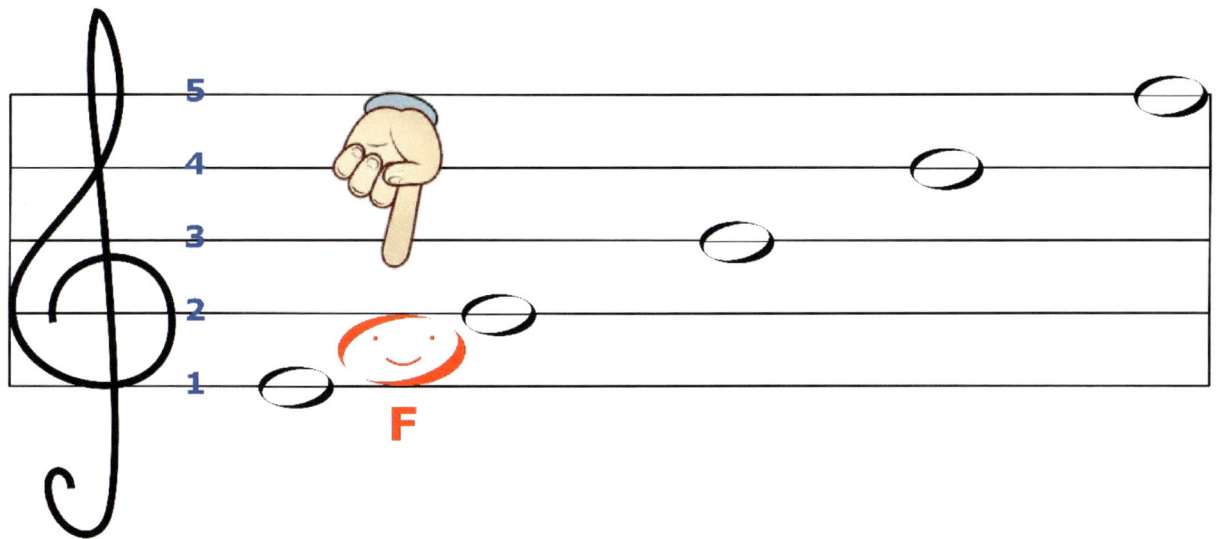

and between them lives note "F." Her apartment is between the first and second line. Do you see? She shows her face! I wrote it in red, so you could clearly see her. And now I will write the name of this note at the bottom.

Next, be careful: Between the notes, which are written on the second and third line, we will write a note "A."

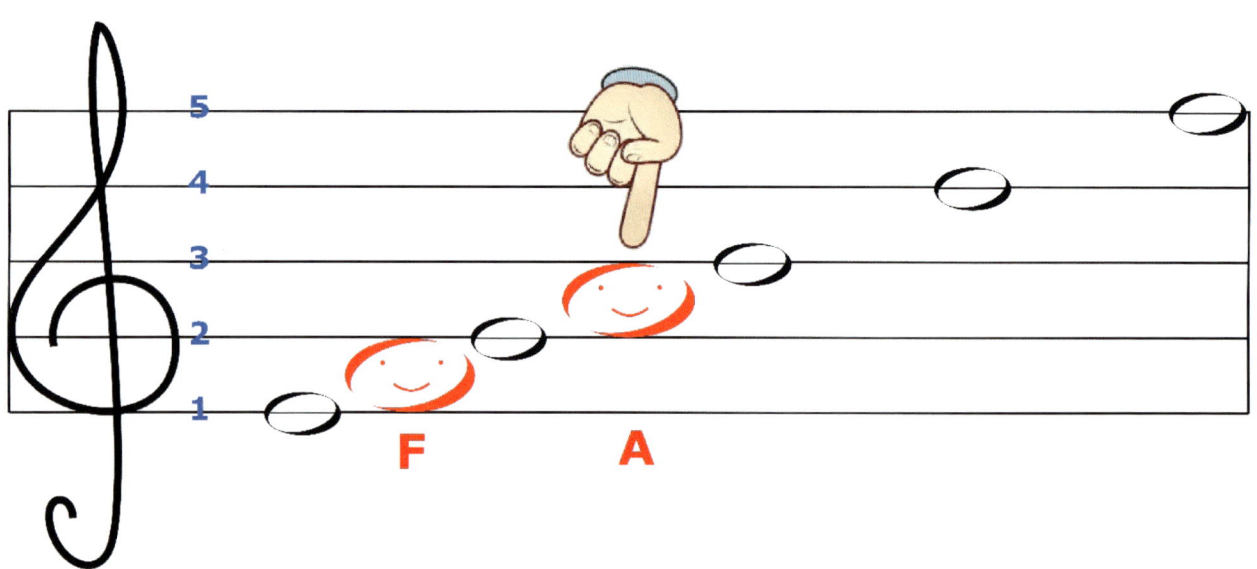

Now, between the notes, which are written on the third and the fourth line, we write the note "C."

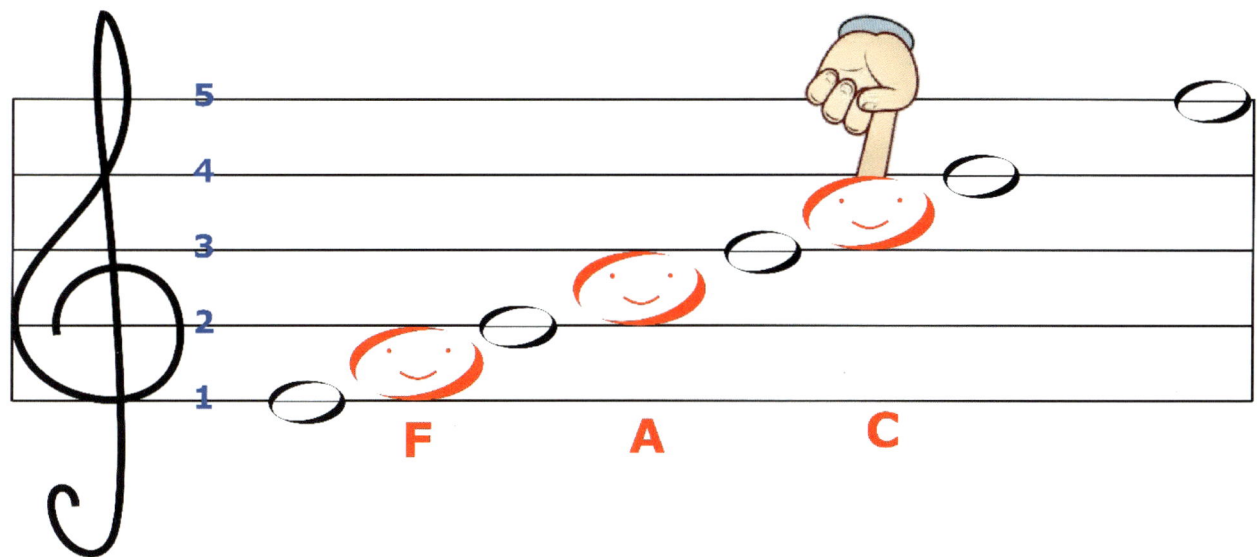

And, finally, between the notes on the fourth and fifth lines we will put a note "E."

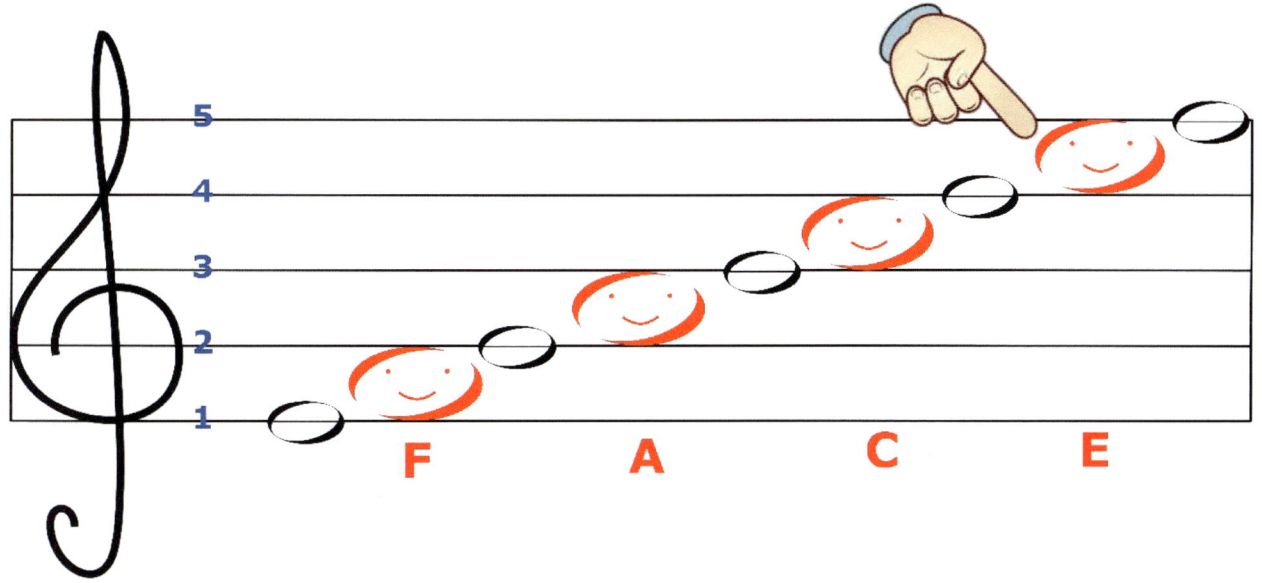

Look what we have: The note on the line, the note between lines, on the line, between the lines, on the line, between the lines, etc.

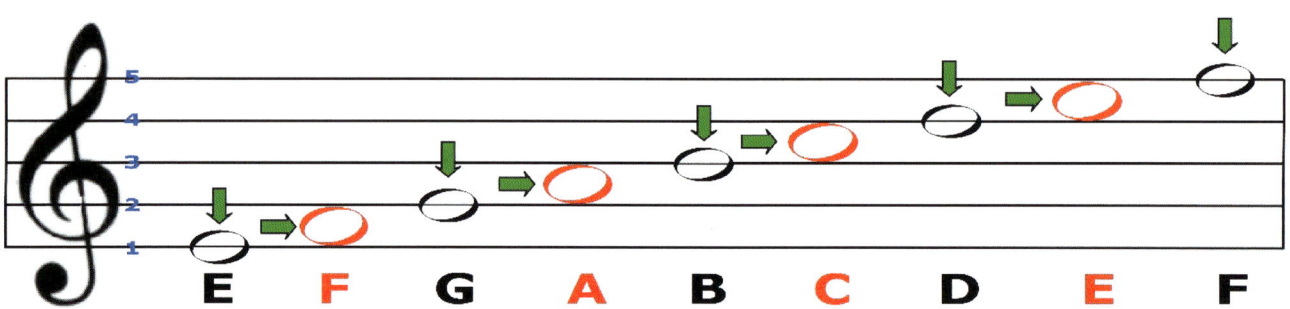

Now you know that the musical notes are written on the lines and between them!

So we put things in order in our musical house, repopulating it completely. When you handle the resettlement of notes on the staff yourself, then you can take on the position of a musical manager in your magical musical house!

And then all the members of your family should call you "Mr. Musical Manager."

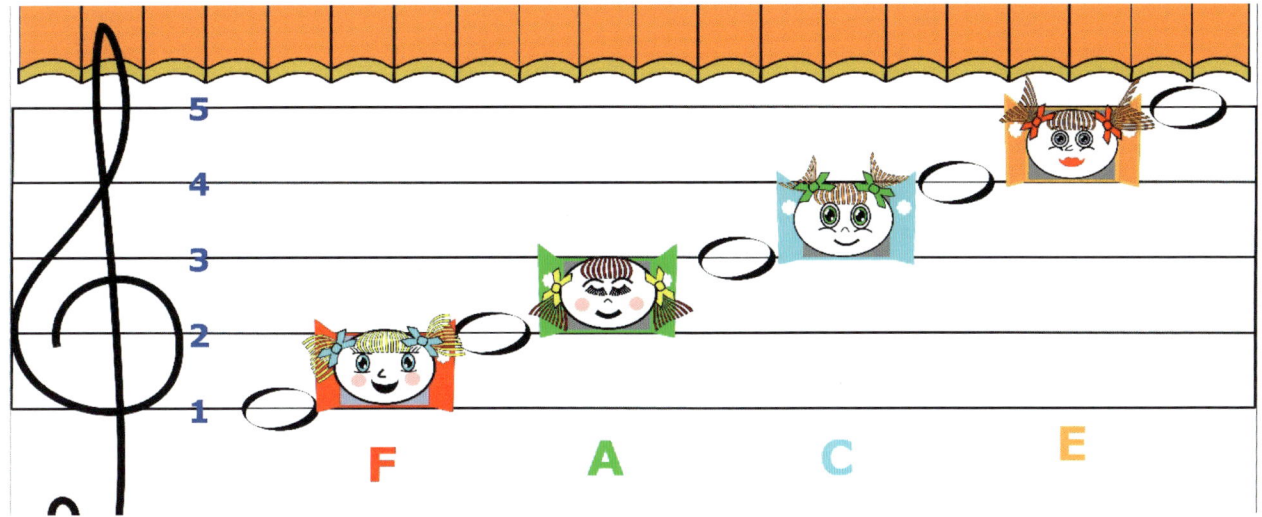

But not so fast! In order to obtain this high rank, you have to convince everyone that you know how to settle notes on the staff as well, as it makes the best manager in a large five-story building.

To do this, you should tell everyone you know about the story of the musical notes that settled between floors and constantly poke their faces through the windows to show their neighbors. Remember what they are called? Why do they have such names?

Well, if you manage to write all the notes on the lines and between the lines in the correct order, but still do it in a marker or pen of the same color, then everyone will just have to call you "Sir Main Music Manager!"

See you next time and I'll tell you story about two musical zebras!

Bye, bye!

HOMEWORK FOR PARENTS

So, today your child was acquainted with notes that are written between the lines.

Read this story to your son or daughter several times before going on to the written exercises. If your child does not understand, tell him the story using a puppet toy to write notes on the lines and between them. It will attract the attention of your son or daughter and will flame their interest. Then, give the toy to the child and ask him to repeat what you have written. Show how your dog (cat, bear, etc.) is able to write notes on the lines and between them!

To see how well your child remembers the content of the story, ask him a few questions. Searching for the answers to questions is a great way to learn! It develops concentration and focus in the child's memory, as well as the ability to separate the important things from the secondary.

Start your training with the question of what the notes from the beauty salon called their friendship union. If the child does not remember, then ask him what the notes were doing in the beauty salon. Possible answers:

Notes painted eyes. (Ask: Where are the eyes? - On the face!)

More notes painted lips. (Ask: Where are the lips? - On the face.)

More notes painted their cheeks to make them rosy. (Ask: Where are the cheeks? - On the face!)

Notes painted eyebrows. (Where are the eyebrows?)

And a note powdered what? (A face!)

Write the word FACE in large letters on a sheet of paper, each time saying the word FACE; show it to the child.

When a child successfully copes with the questions about the notes in the beauty salon, ask him: Why did the beauty notes want to live in a musical home? (Answer: They wanted to show their beautiful faces to the neighbors!)

And now let your child tell you where the notes from the beauty salon settled within the musical house. How did this happen?

If you are satisfied with the answers your son or daughter gives, then now is the time for practical training. If the child is confused about the answers and cannot answer more than 50% of all the questions in a lesson, the next time you read this story, do it with a few pauses along the way, asking questions to ascertain how closely he listens to you.

For practical training, *Blank Music Sheets for Kids* are the best, which you can buy here: www.amazon.com/dp/1483946703

This collection is quite popular, as each page looks funny, so your child will enjoy spending time writing down notes on a staff.

The main advantage of this book is that the staves on the sheets for writing practice have varying widths between lines. This is not done by accident. The fact is that, for a young child, it is very difficult to write notes of a standard size on a staff. Only some children can successfully cope with this difficult task. That's why, for this purpose, I suggest you purchase *Blank Music Sheets for Kids*. *Blank Music Sheets for Kids*-a good start for beginners who want to learn to write musical notes and melodies!

Important!

Always start new practical training only when your child is free to focus on the themes of previous lessons. It's impossible to glean new knowledge to learn new skills well without the previous base.

So, before the eyes of your little one is a music sheet or *Blank Music Paper for Kids*. Where to start?

Let him write all the notes on the lines that he knows and sign their names (repetition—the mother of learning).

LITTLE MUSIC LESSONS FOR KIDS:
FIVE SWEET STORIES ABOUT THE MUSICAL NOTES, PIANO KEYBOARD, TREBLE CLEF AND MUSICAL STAFF

Then let the child write all the notes between the lines he has learned in this lesson. Help him to identify every note with a correct letter.

Now ask your young musician to write notes on the lines again and leave enough space between them (for the space notes).

Only then should you ask your child to write the notes that are written between the lines. For the sake of clarity, let him do it with pencils or markers of different colors so he will more easily see the difference between the notes on the lines and those between them, as well as the distance between the notes.

Keep an eye on the fact that there is little distance between the notes on the lines and between them. Notes do not touch each other!

If the child writes notes that "stick" to each other, you can make a joke:

"Look! Your notes are smeared with glue and stick together! How will they walk, play and go to the store now? Let's help them free themselves. Write all the notes again!"

After that job, pay attention to your child to ensure that the location of the notes on the staff alternates in the order:

- Note on the line

- Note between lines

- Note on the line

- Note between lines

- Note on the line

- Note between lines

- Note on the line

- Note between lines

- Note on the line

How quickly will your child cope with this task? It depends on many factors—the age of your child, his visual memory, eye-hand coordination and other skills. Here's what you need to know: Never begin to learn new material until your child has consolidated the previous learning. Therefore, if the child cannot write on the same staff, notes on the lines should go in one color and notes between the lines should go in a different color, and you should let him write it up separately:

Only the notes on the lines

Only the notes between the lines

When your child is able to easily cope with this task, give him the job of writing all of the notes (two colors) on a single staff.

When a child can easily cope with this task, complicate it!

To do this, ask them to write all the notes in a pencil of the same color. This work can be done in two ways:

1. Write down notes on the lines, leaving enough space between them, and then enter the notes that are written between the rulers. (That is what your child was doing with pencils of different colors).

2. Write down notes using the same color in order:

On the line

Between lines

On the line

Between lines

On the line

And so on...

For some children, it is difficult to accommodate all of the notes with the same distance between them during the first session. To do this they need additional training.

There is a very simple pedagogical device to stimulate your child to practice more (no extra pressure on him!). After he writes all the notes, say, in black, ask the child to write these notes in red, then yellow, then blue, etc.

Once your son (or daughter) shows what he did, be sure to praise his work! For example:

"Your red notes look much prettier than the blue. They are so neat and independent! Do you see? They are in the correct order and none of the notes stick to another! Just perfect! Good for you! Now let's see how orange notes will look. Maybe you would prefer to write a note in a different color? Which one? Do it!"

Remember

You know your child best of all, so only you can give him the most appropriate tasks. DO NOT rush to implement all work in one session. Your session should be 10-20 minutes long. If you push your son or daughter to learn and practice, they can lose interest for a long time or even forever. Always try to play (not learn!) with a child.

Follow the recommendation of this lesson and decide for yourself when to stop.

Once a child learns to write the notes with the correct distance between them and using the same color pencil, the main goal of writing notes on the staff has been achieved. Now you can start exploring writing entire tunes.

For this purpose, I recommend teaching your child to distinguish the note names, time values, time signatures and music melodies in the music books, and only then to write them yourself.

In the sixth lesson of the series Little Music Lessons for Kids, your child will be acquainted with the length of notes. This is a truly amazing story about a singing apple and an angry knife that you can tell and show to your child right in the kitchen!

ISBN-13: 978-1494393700

ISBN-10: 1494393700

Little Music Lessons for Kids

Lesson 5
Learning the Piano Keyboard
Old Story about Two Musical Zebras

Tatiana Bandurina

CONTENTS

Hi! It's me again, the musical puppy.

Do you know what the piano is? It is a very famous musical instrument. Have you ever seen its keyboard? Do you remember what color keys it has?

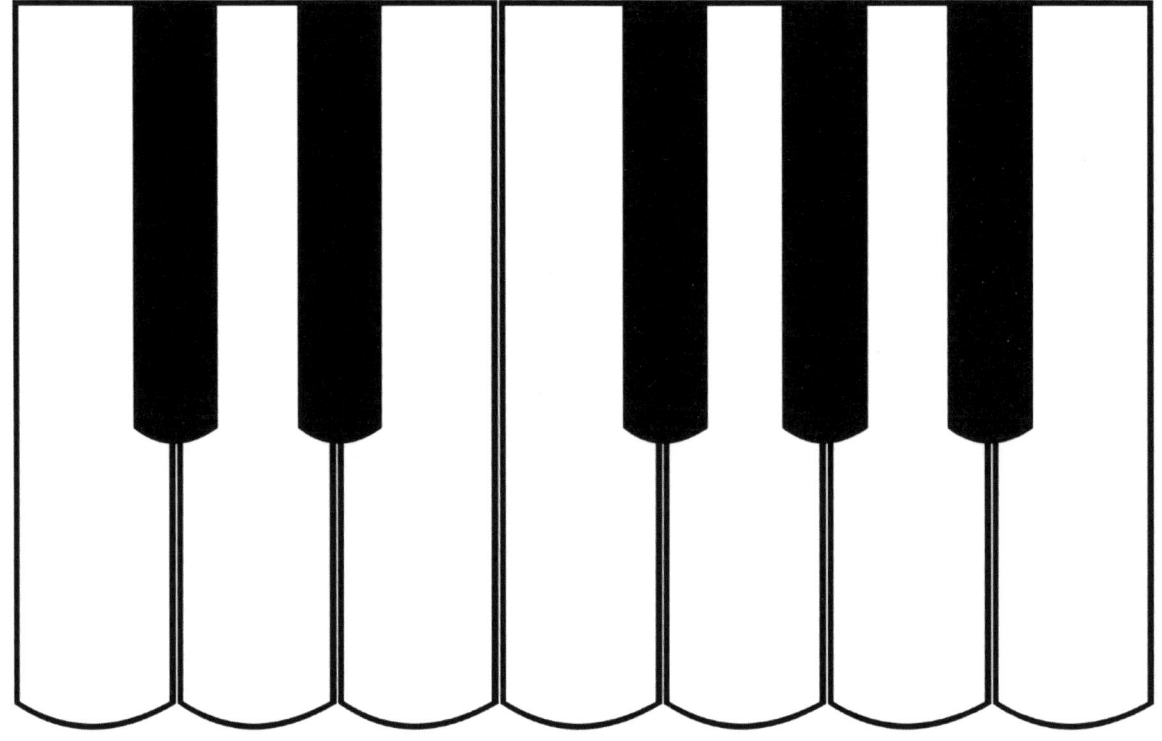

Yes, you are right - white and black.

Maybe you know, my little friend, how the piano keyboard was created? One day, two fabulous zebras suggested an idea to their musical master…

Wait, you do not know? Then listen to this very old musical story.

Once upon a time, there was a small zebra.

She looked like a striped horse; she had been painted with white and black stripes. And, if you looked closely, you could see the same picture on the whole zebra; it was on her hips, legs and even her face.

What was this picture? It was three white and two black stripes. Look closely at the little zebra and you'll see it.

The little zebra was named C D E.

The zebra liked walking in the forest, singing songs and smelling the flowers. She had composed a song about herself and repeated it all the time:

"I am zebra C D E, C D E, C D E

I like walking C D E, C D E, C D E!"

One day, the little zebra found a large forest clearing and was very happy.

"How nice! I can walk through this glade all day and won't run into the big trees and shrubs!"

And the little zebra began to walk in circles, lifting her feet high, and singing her favorite song:

"I am zebra C D E, C D E, C D E

I like walking C D E, C D E, C D E."

At the same time, on the other side of the clearing, a second zebra was standing. She was hidden behind a large tree trunk. This zebra was bigger and older than our little zebra. The large zebra watched the small zebra with amazement and did not dare to approach her.

Finally, the large zebra plucked up the courage and left her hiding place.

"Hey!" said the little zebra in a friendly manner. "My name is C D E and I like walking. Do you like walking?"

"No," said the big zebra, confused.

"What do you like most of all?" asked the little zebra.

"Most of all?" The large zebra repeated the question and thought a bit. Then the big zebra smiled and said:

"Most of all, I love to jump!"

"You bet!" exclaimed the little zebra. "You have such long legs! I also love to jump, but I like to walk more because I have short legs. What is your name?"

The large zebra stared at the little zebra and said nothing to her.

The little Zebra thought that she spoke too softly for the zebra on her long legs to hear her, so she repeated the question loudly and articulately:

"WHAT IS YOUR NA-ME?"

"I do not know ..." said large zebra, softly.

"Really? You do not know?" The little zebra was surprised. "All zebras have names and they are written on their bodies!"

The large zebra was silent, and the little zebra kept saying:

"Look at me!"

She showed her right side. "Do you see those three white stripes, and the two black on them? The names of these three white stripes are CDE. This is MY name! I even have a song! Just listen:

"I am zebra C D E, C D E, C D E

I like walking C D E, C D E, C D E."

When the little zebra had finished singing, she continued talking:

"And you have four white and three black stripes. Read!"

Hearing the cheerful song of the little zebra, the big zebra started crying, loudly.

Zebra C D E was surprised. She had never seen big zebras crying. She guessed that the large zebra could not read and began to comfort her:

"Do not cry! I'm too small and cannot read the names of other zebras, but we can ask someone! Look, the elephant is coming our way. I am sure that he knows how to read. Do not worry; we'll know your name very soon!"

The elephant came to a clearing to eat fresh, green grass. His mouth was full of young leaves. The elephant stood and slowly chewed.

Zebra C D E cautiously approached the elephant and asked:

"Dear elephant, would you be so kind as to help us to read out the name on this zebra?"

Thoroughly chewing and swallowing all the grass and leaves, the elephant replied politely:

"I'm sorry, ladies, but I left my glasses at home and cannot read anything now. So, please come tomorrow and I'll help you." The elephant continued to eat the grass.

Hearing the elephant's answer, the large zebra sobbed louder.

Zebra C D E comforted her as best as she could.

The loud crying of the big zebra woke an owl. She began to worry:

"What is it? Who is crying so loudly and why?"

Zebra C D E ran up to the owl and said:

"Hello, darling owl! This is a big zebra crying. She does not know her name. Her name is written on her hips, legs and face, but neither the elephant nor I could read it!

"Bring her here," said the owl, calmly.

Zebra C D E wiped the large zebra's tears and pushed her in the direction of the tree on which the owl sat.

"Turn around!" commanded the owl. "Once again, turn around! More ... More ..."

The owl blinked and then puffed out her eyes, straining to see something.

"No, excuse me, girls, there is too much light here. I cannot read anything. Come to me at night and I'll help you."

The large zebra began to sob again, but the owl interrupted her crying. She commanded:

"Quiet! Do you hear?"

"What do we need to hear?" asked the large zebra, sobbing.

"There is a nightingale singing!" said the owl.

"So what?" asked C D E.

"That's who will help you!" exclaimed the owl.

"You are the smartest in the forest, but could not help me. Elephant, the largest in our forest, couldn't help me either. How is a little bird able to help me?" asked the big zebra in surprise.

"The nightingale is the best singer. He knows the musical notes and says that zebras bear not only the musical notes' names, but the whole tunes!"

"So he can read the white and black stripes?" asked the small zebra; her voice sounded full of hope.

"Best of all!" confirmed the owl.

"Run to the Nightingale!" cried the big zebra, joyfully. She quickly jumped to the side, trying to follow the bird's song. Zebra CDE followed her.

Coming to another forest glade, the two zebras saw a small bird whistling a beautiful melody.

The Nightingale sang so well that the zebras almost forgot why they had gone there. Finally, the little bird stopped singing when she saw her guests. After a short pause, she filled her lungs with air and sang again, looking at the zebras:

"C D E, C D E

F G A B, F G A B"

"Did you hear? He sang my name!" cried zebra C D E, joyfully.

"Yes, but he sang something else!" the large zebra excitedly confirmed. "I think he sang: F G A B, F G A B."

"That's right!" confirmed the nightingale. "It's written on your face, side, on your right front leg and in general—everywhere."

"Hooray!" cried the big zebra, jumping for joy. "My name is F G A B!"

"Oh! You like to jump?" asked the nightingale.

"Yes, very much!" admitted the lucky F G A B. "And I also want to have my own song like C D E has."

"Well," said the nightingale, "Then repeat after me: I am zebra F G A B, F G A B, F G A B."

The large zebra repeated:

"I am zebra F G A B, F G A B, F G A B."

"I like jumping F G A B, F G A B, F G A B," continued the nightingale.

"I like jumping F G A B, F G A B, F G A B," repeated the zebra again.

"Now jump and sing!" commanded the nightingale.

Big zebra was keen to implement this command.

"Well, now you have a song too!" said C D E gladly and started singing and walking across the meadow:

"I am zebra C D E, C D E, C D E

I like walking C D E, C D E, C D E."

"I am zebra F G A B, F G A B, F G A B,

I like jumping F G A B, F G A B, F G A B," sang the large zebra, leaping and following the small one.

At the same time, a master of musical instruments watched the two zebras' game. He wanted to create a new musical instrument, but could not find suitable ideas for it. Seeing the two musical zebras play, he couldn't take his eyes off them.

"Come on, get together!" said the nightingale, "First the little zebra and then the big one. That's it!" The nightingale sang again:

"C D E F G A B, C D E F G A B."

"Eureka!" exclaimed the master of musical instruments, drawing a piano keyboard.

And that's the story about how the piano keyboard was created.

Do you like this story? Great! Next time, I'll tell you a new story about a wonderful apple that loved to sing, and about the angry knife that loved to cut.

Bye, bye!

HOMEWORK FOR PARENTS

This story can be read (or told) to children regardless of their musical knowledge and abilities. You do not need to comply with the chronological order that you should follow in the first four music lessons in the series Little Music Lessons for Kids—1st, 2nd, 3rd, 4th—yet, this lesson is very important at the beginning of teaching music to children.

Whatever musical instrument your child chooses in the future, he will have to get acquainted with the piano. Most of the time, the piano is selected as a complementary instrument if your child is enrolled in a music school. There are subjects such as elementary music, theory and harmony that are essential for anyone who wants to get a musical education. By studying these subjects, your child will just need to know the piano keyboard. That's why I included this lesson in the series Little Music Lessons for Kids.

Thus, all children will easily pay attention to the contrasting color of the piano keys, and may even notice that the two black keys alternate with three other black keys.

Once the child has learned the location of the notes on the staff, he can proceed to the next phase of training. Now he must find the familiar notes on the keyboard and one of the first challenges begins here.

The notes on the lines and spaces between them are already very familiar to the child, but "in real life" they look completely different.

But there is good news! The challenge of associating the theory with the positioning of notes on a keyboard develops not only musical and physical abilities in your child, but also mental abilities. The child improves coordination between the eyes and hands, and his brain learns to quickly switch from one type of activity (reading notes) to a completely different one (clicking on the keys in order to extract sounds). In modern terms, the musical notes are converting within the child's head into the keys on a piano.

We can easily see that two black keys alternate with three other black keys, but how will your child easily and quickly learn to navigate the white keys?

To make this difficult task easier, I came up with the story of the two zebras. Usually children easily remember not only the content of the story, but the names of heroes and their songs. This is exactly what you need for your child!

As you read this story, focus your child's attention on the black and white keys, written on zebras. Let him count the white keys that correspond to the small zebra and the large zebra.

As you read the story the second or third time, touch the white keys yourself whilst saying their names. Once the child learns both zebras' songs, let him "click" on the white keys (white stripes on a zebra) and say their names.

If your child is small and it is difficult for them to remember the names of the keys while reading the book, then proceed to action!

Children learn faster when they play, so use the zebras' songs in games with the child. Ask what was the most loved activity for the little zebra? That's right, to walk! Let's walk like a little zebra!

Set an example: first you begin to walk, raising your feet and reading a poem:

I am zebra C D E, C D E, C D E

I like walking C D E, C D E, C D E.

When a child knows the song of the big zebra, do the same thing by not just walking, but leaping. Then assign roles, and say: Now you're the little zebra, and I will be the big zebra!

After a while, you can then change roles with your child.

When the child knows the two zebras' songs well, ask him to create music zebras with his hands!

Important!

Never do the work that your child can do himself! When he does something for the first time, do not interfere. Do not rush to make suggestions. It's better to see whether or not he is able to come up with the answers himself. The more you involve your child in the tasks personally, the faster he will develop his skills, acquire new experiences and, therefore, increase his interest in learning-because he will appreciate his own achievements!

Making Zebras with Our Hands

To make musical zebras, buy white glue, wooden sticks in two sizes (wide for the white keys and narrow for the black). Also purchase scissors, black and white paint and a brush (if you do not already have them). Make all of the above purchases in advance.

When the necessary "building" material is ready, give your child the whole pack of wide wooden sticks and ask him to count seven of them and put them on a white sheet of paper (A4 will suffice). If the child makes a mistake during counting, just ask him to count the sticks once again.

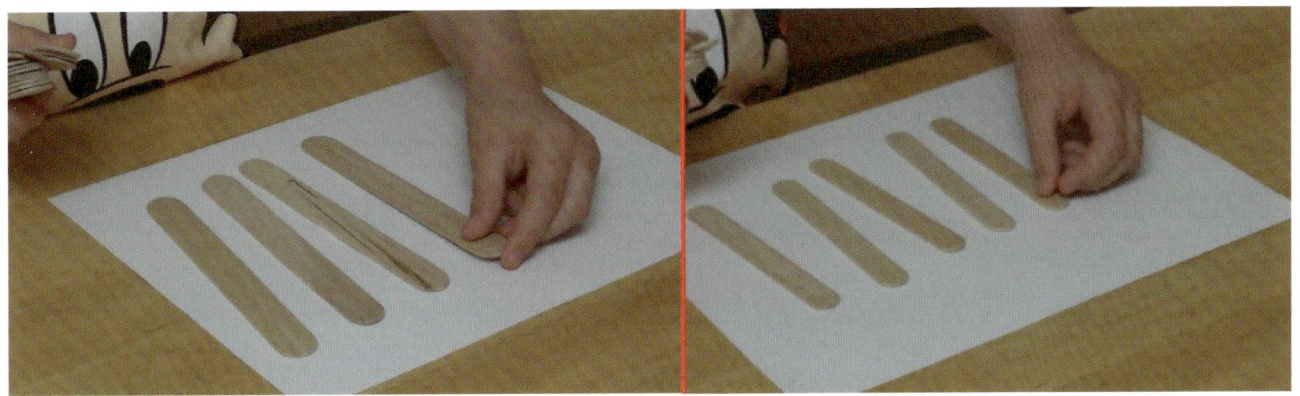

When the wide sticks are correctly counted and laid out, give the child the whole pack of narrow wooden sticks and ask him to count five of them and also put them on another sheet of white paper.

Prepare the white paint and ask your child to paint the broad sticks in white. Then do the same with the narrow sticks.

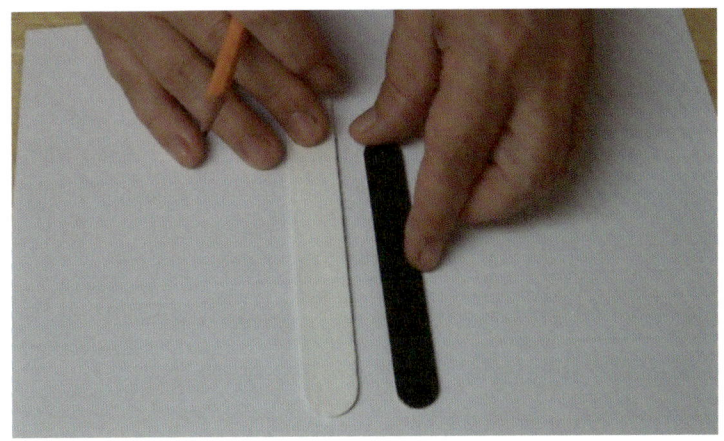

When all the components of your future "zebras" have dried, cut the black sticks. Their length should be half that of the white sticks (or just over half). Now you are ready to create zebras! To do this, you need two sheets of white A4 paper (one for the little zebra, the other for the large zebra) and white glue.

Again, try to help your child as little as possible in the attaching of keys to the paper. Allow your child to do this work himself. You can adjust a key if it is crooked.

Please ask your child to divide all the keys into two parts. He must count the three white and two black keys for a small zebra. Have the child put them on a single sheet of paper. Let your child check the number of white and black keys for a large zebra and put them on another sheet of paper.

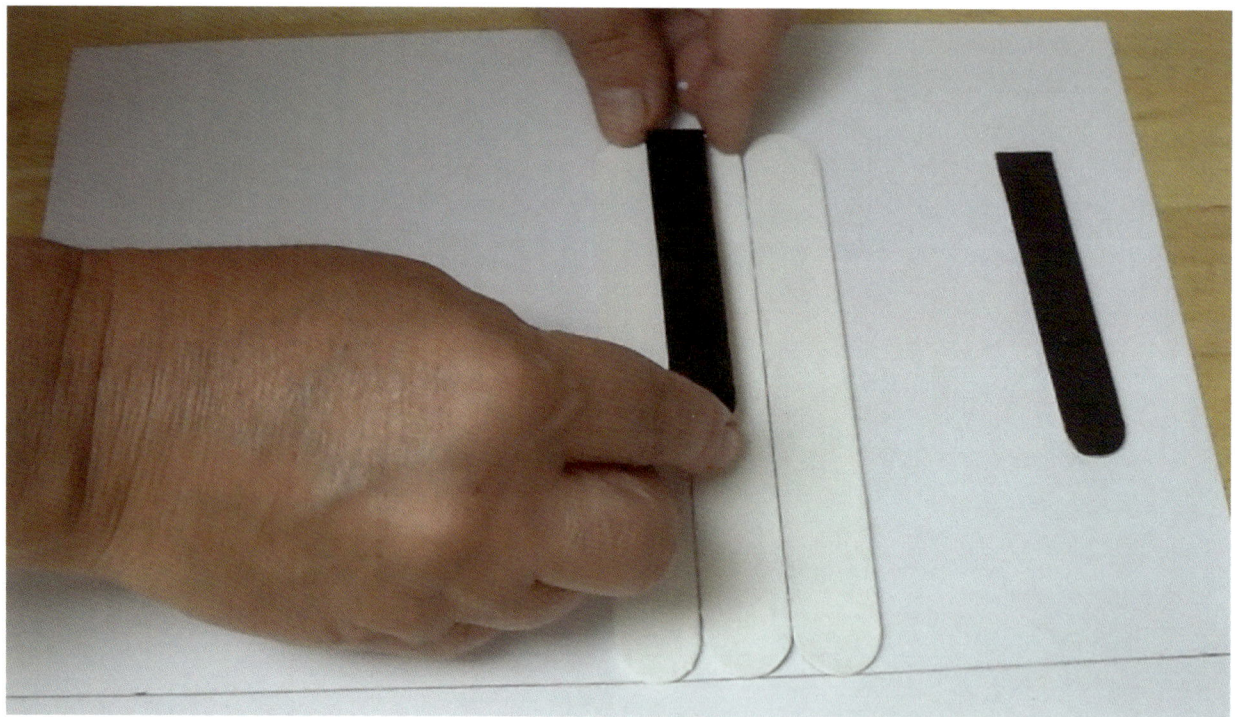

Start with the small zebra. Your son or daughter should glue three white keys first, placing them next to one another. To make a "zebra" look flat, you can draw a straight line on the paper and ask them to attach keys to it. Then let the child glue the black keys in between the white, as shown on a zebra in this book. Put a picture of a zebra in front of him if he does not remember the exact location of the black key strips.

While the small "zebra" dries, you can start making the second part of the keyboard-a big "zebra." Now your child should glue four white keys and three black keys on a piece of paper.

After the "zebras" dry up, you can take a pair of scissors and cut off the excess paper. Your musical zebras are ready! Let's play!

Assign roles: Who will be the big zebra and who will be the little zebra? Sing the songs one by one, and then reverse the roles. During the performance of the songs, list the names of the white keys and touch them with your finger.

While playing, put the "zebras" together, small and large. Swap their places so that the large comes first, followed by the small.

Attention!

Never write the names of the notes on the white keys! Let the child remember them immediately (without transition) in the same way that, if you wanted to learn a foreign language, such as the language of another galaxy, and decided to extend your vocabulary, you would visually memorize the word as it is written in the new language. But if you wrote an unknown word in characters from your native alphabet, then remembering it would take much longer. Same goes for musical grammar. If your child learns to memorize the keys straight away (without additional inscriptions), this skill will give him a great leap forward in the development of memory (and not only musical and visual memory). Believe me, in the future, your child will benefit from this skill quite often in other situations (already at a subconscious level).

Repetition-the mother of learning. Play as often as possible with your child and encourage him as he does it. If you have a piano, it's a great idea to find the "zebras" on it and name them by clicking on the white keys. It does not matter if you have a small keyboard, an electronic instrument with keys or a glockenspiel. If they are broken and make no sound, this is not important either at this moment. The main thing is that your child learns the location of the keys and learns to focus on the keyboard.

If you do not have a suitable musical instrument for practice, make two more "zebras" and connect the four "zebras" together-a small zebra, then a large one, then small, and then large-and practice on your own keyboard.

When your child knows the names of the keys pretty well, complicate the exercises and suggest a more difficult game:

Touch the keys in any order (not in succession like in the song) and ask your child to name these keys. First, touch the keys slowly, giving the child time to think, to understand and get used to the new game mode. Then, touch the keys faster and faster. Be sure to encourage your child.

In the next lesson, your child will hear a compelling story about an apple that loved to sing about the angry knife that liked to cut everything he sees. With the help of this fairy tale, your son or daughter will learn the length of notes.

HANDWRITING FOR KIDS – PRACTICE WORKSHEETS

Blank Music Paper for Kids

Your child will like this colorful Blank Music Paper for Kids. Each page looks very funny, and they'll attract the attention of your child. You can download this file on your PC and print out or buy colored printed blank music papers that are ready to use.

Blank Music Paper for Kids has 27 pages and will make the hard practice of your child in musical notation easier. All pages are designed for children who are just start learning music and want to practice how to write musical clefs, notes, rests and other musical signs.

There is different quantity of the staffs in manuscripts.

Manuscripts with three staffs: The width between lines of the staffs has comfortable space for little kids (three-four years old). They are also for any beginners without experience.

Manuscripts with four and five staffs are for children who have a bit experience in writing musical notation.

Help your child to get fun instead of boring practice!

Available on Amazon

Music Lessons Planer for Girls

Music Lessons Planner For Girls

40 Weeks Music Student's Organizer

Your girl can use this very comfortable Music Lessons Planner for any grades, musical instruments or voice training. There is enough space on each side of the planner where the music teacher will leave detailed instruction for the student's homework after each lesson. If your girl is visiting chorus, orchestra or ensemble, she can easily write and track all tasks, works and activities in this organizer. This organizer is for the students who are learning in music schools or have private teachers. This Music Lessons Planner can be used for 40 weeks.

Available on Amazon

Music Lessons Planer for Boys

Music Lessons Planner for Boys

40 Weeks Music Student's Organizer

To better organize your boy's music education we recommend this music lessons planner. Each student can use this organizer for 40 weeks of studying in music school or with a private music teacher. Here is how it can help your child: after each lesson the music teacher can leave detailed instructions for the student's homework. The child can actively manage his time, set goals and work towards them. If your boy is visiting chorus, orchestra or ensemble, he can track all tasks in this comfortable organizer and develop strong academic skills. Can be used for any grades, musical instruments or voice training.

Available on Amazon

CPSIA information can be obtained at www.ICGtesting.com
Printed in the USA
LVIW01n1445200815
450914LV00004B/49

* 9 7 8 1 4 9 4 3 9 3 7 0 0 *